Peter Gibson

A BOOK OF SUPERSTITIONS

by the same author

A BOOK OF EPITAPHS
A BOOK OF PROVERBS
A BOOK OF WITCHCRAFT

A BOOK
OF
SUPERSTITIONS

by
RAYMOND LAMONT BROWN

*

Line whimsies by Ernest Petts

DAVID & CHARLES : NEWTON ABBOT

New impression printed by Redwood Press Ltd
Set in 10 point Plantin 2 point leaded
and originally printed in Great Britain
by Latimer Trend & Company Limited
for David & Charles (Publishers) Limited
South Devon House Newton Abbot Devon

Contents

  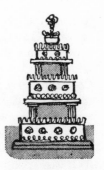

I

Sources of Superstition

When lightning flashed and thunder roared across vale and mountain in ancient times, our ancestors petitioned favours of Odin, most powerful of all the Norse gods, and omniscient ruler of heaven and earth. Whether in Britain or Gaul, Sweden or Norway, while ordinary folk in their rude huts and shelters quaked in fear of the elements, the wise ones stood on high cliffs and ledges, faces white with ecstasy, bodies bedecked with bones and painted with symbols, to hear the wishes and instructions of the gods, or to try to direct lesser spirits themselves. Such ideas have possessed the mind of man since Neolithic and Megalithic times.

Originally meaning 'a standing still in apprehension or awe', superstition is a belief, or system of beliefs, by which almost religious veneration is attached to things mostly secular; a parody of religious faith in which there is belief in an occult or magic connection.

7

Every religion has tended to accumulate superstitions, until the word has now, ambiguously, come to include peripheral beliefs. Caius Cornelius Tacitus (55–*circa* 120), for instance, said that Christianity was a pernicious superstition, while Constantine (*circa* 272–337), Emperor of Rome, called paganism superstition. Christians would regard aboriginal totem worship as superstition, while those same aboriginals might equally well look upon the veneration of Christian saints' relics as superstition.

Superstitions which belong to cultural tradition are infinite in their variety and importance, and many have deeply influenced world history, including the development and retardation of scientific knowledge. Today, as it has been from the dawn of time, man's superstitions have taken three definite forms. The first is the prohibition, or taboo, in which it is believed that actions taken will provoke evil spirits, or in a more modern sense, ill-luck will ensue.

In the past, to speak a name was enough to summon misfortune; even as the ancient Egyptians believed that mention of the name of a dead Pharaoh could make him live again. The idea is often reflected in folk rhyme, as with this example from Scotland:

> Gin ye ca' me imp or elf,
> I rede ye look weel tae yerself;
> Gin ye ca' me fairy,
> I'll wark ye muckle tarrie.

From ancient times, then, a man's name was not just a convenient label, but an integral part of himself. It followed that anyone knowing a name could use it, if they had the necessary magic power, to destroy that person. This has passed into the custom, once quite common, of keeping a baby's name secret until baptism. Again, sailors believe that it is unlucky to alter the name of a ship, or to give one a name, like the *Lusitania*, which ends in 'A'.

The second form of superstition is the ritual in which a

sequence of events brings about desired effects. The third concerns omens—the portents and forewarnings by which, it is claimed, a specific result may be expected. Such a belief is based on a predetermined future, totally fatalistic, in the way that finding money or meeting a black cat may be taken as good-luck signs.

Similarly, the startling brilliance of the light in the Aurora Borealis brought primitive people to their knees in supplication, fervently praying to the god of war to avert disaster. These lights have often been attributed to an impending rebellion; Henry the Chronicler in the *Acts of Stephen* recorded how heavenly light appeared before the Huntingdon rebellion of 1138, and a similar case was cited in Northumberland before the 1715 Stuart rebellion. Not forgetting, of course, the famous example in the Bayeux Tapestry of the appearance of Halley's Comet in July 1066. 'Then over all England there was seen a sign in the skies such as had never been seen before. Some said it was the "star" (comet) which some call "the star with hair",' records the *Anglo-Saxon Chronicle*; and on the tapestry is seen a group of men (*isti mirant stella*—these men wonder at the star) staring up at the comet, together with a very worried-looking King Harold II who, as events were to prove, had good reason to be worried! And in our own time, curiously enough, brilliant displays of nature's electricity were recorded over Michigan and Ohio just before the disastrous attack on Pearl Harbour in World War II.

During ages in which men of one faction have questioned the beliefs of those of another, even to the point of making war, or whenever there has been a new upsurge of knowledge and invention, man's mind seems to have slipped back within itself to the primitive credulity of his ancestors.

For instance, the carefully built structural dogmas of post-sixteenth-century Europe concerning the universe and man's place in it began to crack during the mid-1550s and by the seventeenth century had started to crumble. The result was that

9

ordinary men and women were thrown into a wilderness of doubt and frantically sought comfort in the things with which they were familiar and had lived alongside all their lives. Superstition developed from this bewildernment and uncertainty, and wandered in their minds like unconnected atoms.

Today, with the imminence of interplanetary travel, the shadow of another world war and the phenomenal growth of knowledge, we, too, are almost as perplexed and frightened as our sixteenth=century kinsmen and are drifting towards a new manifestation of superstition, which may have already begun. Libraries' and publishers' lists show the increased interest in books on magic and the occult which springs from feelings of doubt and subconscious fear, or even the conscious desire to improve one's lot by means other than the natural.

Nevertheless, the study of superstitions is of great importance to the social historian and psychologist alike, for they reflect thought patterns of very ancient times; beliefs once tenaciously held which are now either forgotten, changed completely, or but remnant shadows in the mind.

Carefully assessed, superstitions throw light on the history of our ethnic groups and help us to understand the thought processes of our ancestors in relation to our own. While some superstitions seem ridiculous today they have, in fact, only been supplanted by others; today the superstitions once shadowing the cradle and the broomstick now appear in connection with the baby-carriage and the camera. For even photographs have now been given occult attributes, and only recently two football teams from Devon refused to have their photographs taken before a match in case it brought them bad luck. Photographs, too, have been used to break witches' spells, much as the clay and wood dolls of the past were utilised, and it is on record that only forty years ago in Wiltshire, a witch was cursed to death using a photograph. Witchcraft, in fact, only ceased to be a crime in Britain as late as 1951.

Thus many ancient superstitions have laid the basis for

modern beliefs and prejudices, but whereas the actions of our ancestors were rational in relation to their beliefs in good and evil, ours are completely irrational in the light of the modern interpretation of Christianity and science.

Superstitious rituals are also still very much alive. At Zurich, in Switzerland, in January 1969, six members of a sect were found guilty of 'beating the devil' out of a girl, and at Cambridge, Massachusetts, around the same time, police found the murdered corpse of a twenty-three-year-old co-ed sprinkled with red ochre—an essential practice in centuries' old burial rites to ensure the dead a safe entrance to paradise.

Again in Zambia in 1969, some Asiatic *ngungus* (medicine-men) escaped the axe of internal economic reforms because it was feared they might put spells upon their Zambian replacements, or cast evil shadows over President Kaunda's Government. And President Nyerere of the nearby United Republic of Tanzania is also on record as saying, 'I am a good, superstitious African. And I believe in devils.' And not only the once 'Dark Continent', modern 'big business' can also be influenced by superstition, and at least one British firm is known to employ an astrologer to forecast the most favourable times for business deals.

In the USA, the first day of January 1951 saw the formation of a corporation known as Water Unlimited. Headed by novelist Kenneth Roberts, this group was convinced that one, Henry Gross, possessed supernatural powers for accurate water-divining. (A book *Henry Gross and His Divining* appeared that same year.) Gross was employed by a school board at New Hampshire, a group of Texan cotton growers and such companies as RCA Victor and Bristol-Myers to discover water. The old superstition is that one person in every ten born has the power of finding water by instinct.

For the same reason that Billy Eckstine kept an old trumpet, and tourists throw coins into a fountain at Rome ('Three Coins in the Fountain'), the students at the US Naval Academy still cast coins, before examinations and important games, at the wooden figure of the god Tecumseh. And at Bloomsburg, Pennsylvania, not long ago a thirty-six-year-old unemployed labourer shot and critically wounded a neighbour because he believed that she had 'put a hex (witch's spell)' on him.

Certainly, superstition is as rife today as it ever was; in the USA alone it is estimated that about $130,000,000 are spent each year on superstitious devices, such as good-luck charms. So much so that according to the *Chicago Daily Tribune* of 13 June 1958 'one hundred stalwart men and their guests met at the Chicago Athletic Club to scorn the humbug of superstition, particularly that associated with Friday the 13th. (It is estimated that about $275,000,000 of business is lost on this day in the USA by people staying at home rather than risk emerging on this "unlucky day").'

Under the leadership of Ben Regan, these members of the Anti-Superstition Society, composed of 'aldermen, judges, and leaders of the business and industrial community', with thirteen vice-presidents, defied the bad-luck spells associated with broken mirrors, black cats, ladders, umbrellas and so on. All of which simply goes to prove the continuing accuracy of what Francis Bacon said some 350 years ago, 'In all superstition wise men follow fools.—There is superstition in avoiding superstition'.

Robert B. Thomas, in *The Farmer's Almanack* for 1830, asked questions about superstition:

> Why do you conjure up a thousand frightful monsters to torment yourself, when there are enough of real evils? Some seem to think there is a ghost in every gust of wind. Away with such vain illusions of imagination. Strange it is that a courage that never startles at real dangers should shrink at even the thought of an empty chimera! Signs and omens and prognostions continually fill the mind of some. . . . What power has superstition?'

Today the answer is still the same! IMMENSE!

2

On Amulets and Talismans

Skilled metal workers lived north of the Firth of Forth in Scotland, long before the coming of Christ, their chief occupation being the manufacture of ornaments to ward off evil spirits. Since the Bronze Age the profusion of semi-precious stones to be found in Scotland led to a regular commercial intercourse between Scotland and Ireland, the latter a country rich in superstition from very early times.

To combat the dreaded Evil Eye, Scotland exported stones dipped in sacred peat water and fashioned amulets in great numbers wherever veins of quartz were found among the hills. Eventually, the makers of these 'magic stones' began putting them into special settings, and, from the eighth to the twelfth centuries penannular (ring-shaped) brooches of Celtic ore began to appear, baser metals being replaced by gold and silver from the thirteenth to the sixteenth centuries.

Used as charms against disease and misfortune these amulets,

13

fashioned into brooches, were mostly circular with black engraved inlay. They bore various symbols, or Latin tags like *O Mater Dei momento mei*, or just a simple black M.

One clear rock crystal set in four silver bands with a clasp and chain was the ball-shaped Clach-Dearg of Ardvorlich, considered of matchless might, which belonged to the ancient and venerable family of Stewart of Ardvorlich. All an ill-afflicted person (or animal) had to do for a cure was to drink water in which the stone had been dipped. Often people travelled miles for a carafe of water collected at a dipping ceremony. Said to have been brought from the east by Crusaders, the crystal was used as late as the 1830s for curing animals.

Another of equal powers was the famous brooch of Lorne, a silver disc with a massive socket capped with a huge crystal set inside a crenellated border. Round this were eight turrets each topped with a large pearl. Rumoured to have been a jewel lost by Robert the Bruce at the battle of Dal-Righ, the brooch for many years belonged to the Bragheen Campbells, then became the property of the Macdougals of Dunollie for more than a century.

In Canto II of *Lord of the Isles*, Sir Walter Scott hinted at its mystic potency:

> Whence the brooch of burning gold,
> That clasps the Chieftain's mantle-fold,
> Wrought and chased with rare device,
> Studded fair with gems of price,
> On the varied tartans beaming,
> As, through night's pale rainbow gleaming,
> Fainter now, now seen afar,
> Fitful shines the northern star?
>
> Gem! ne'er wrought on Highland mountain,
> Did the fairy of the fountain,
> Or the mermaid of the wave,
> Frame thee in some coral cave?

> Did, in Iceland's darksome mine,
> Dwarf's swart hands thy metal twine?
> Or mortal-moulded, comest thou here,
> From England's love, or France's fear?

To which Scott added the footnote: 'A studded brooch, said to have been that which King Robert lost upon this occasion, was long preserved in the family of Macdougal, and was lost in a fire which consumed their temporary residence.'

Similar to the brooch of Lorne was that of Lochbuie, alleged to have been made by a *cearden* (tinker, or any itinerant artificer) from silver found on Lochbuie estate on the Island of Mull, in Argyllshire. In 1855 this famous gem was acquired by the British Museum in London.

Large, bulbous and ring-shaped, the Skaill brooches (found in 1858 at Skaill, Orkney) have a mixed parentage. Said to have been struck at Baghdad in 945, they are curiously Viking Jellinge in style, and of the monster design typical of Norse custom.

In time, as Highland warriors began to look down on all types of manual work, the craft of making jewellery and amulets was taken on by the silversmiths of Glasgow and Inverness. Special tokens of goodwill for tradesmen and brooches for lovers were also manufactured in the late seventeenth and eighteenth centuries in lock-up shops, or booths, in Edinburgh High Street, the brooches being known as Luckenbooth Brooches. Usually made of silver, and often in the shape of a heart, or two joined, the design was surmounted by a crown, and the brooches sometimes set with garnets. Although not dipped in sacred water before sale, they were highly regarded by the superstitious and often worn among the clothes on the left thigh because of their efficacy against witches' spells and incantations. Even today these Scottish brooches are still bought in large numbers by tourists and native-born Scots alike as protection against the machinations of the Devil.

Generally small and portable, an amulet may be described as an object which is believed to have a beneficial influence on its owner. A talisman, on the other hand is constructed for a particular purpose, often with an incantation or spell inscribed on it at the most propitious time; the later section on Symbolism mentions some of the many aspects of this superstition.

Ordinary earth was considered to have great magic powers from very ancient times. As the progenitor of all things, it was thought to be more potent when gathered from holy ground, and many people carried dust from a churchyard, or from a place where three lands met, around their necks in a little bag or locket.

Should a man be struck by lightning, to bury him up to his neck in earth was once believed to ensure his rapid recovery, while holy earth made into a plaster was thought, particularly in the West Country of England, to be a sure cure for cancer. Again, in the Shetland Islands, anyone who suffered from stitch was vigorously rubbed with grave mould for swift relief.

Brimstone, too, was well thought of, as we learn from an entry in Parson Woodforde's famous *Diary*:

> I thank God had a better night of rest than I have had the 3 last Nights (27 November 1789). Had no Cramp at all. My Brother recommending me last Night to carry a small Piece of the roll Brimstone sewed up in a piece of very thin Linnen, to bed with me and if I felt any Symptom of the Cramp to hold it in my hand or put it near the affected part, which I did, as I apprehended at one time it was coming into one of my legs, and felt no more advances of it.

With obvious mystical associations with fire and earth, ashes from a hearth were often used in charms and divination. On St Mark's Eve, in Yorkshire, ashes were riddled to try to ascertain who would be the next to die in a household. The ashes were spread on the hearth at bedtime and if, next morning a footprint should be visible in the ash, whosoever's foot fitted the print would be the next to die. Similar beliefs were held in the Isle of Man, and practised in various parts of England on New Year's Eve and at Hallowe'en. Ash gathered from bonfires at Midsummer or Hallowtide was also placed in shoes for good luck, and in Wales it was spread in houses for the same reason.

The Middle Ages saw fresh impetus given to the manufacture of talismans, and there are numerous instances of plates, seals, and cloth pieces being attached to documents, such as conveyances of land, in the belief that they would bring good fortune to those involved in the transactions. A token for a different purpose was attached to a deed sealed by John of Gaunt, Duke of Lancaster (1340–99), son of Edward III and father of Henry IV:

> I, John of Gaunt do give and grant,
> To thee and thine, from me and mine,
> The manor and fee of Umberleigh,
> And in token of my truth do seal it with my tooth.

Again, talismans, or good-luck inscriptions, were often placed on buildings. Over the door at Newbiggen Hall was to be seen:

> Christofer Crakanthorpe thus ye me call
> Which in my tym dyde bylde this hall.
> The yer of our Lord who lyst to see
> A.M. fyve hundred thyrty and three.

In Gloucestershire, a divot of turf worn under the hat acted as a charm against ill-wishing and witchcraft, and in Berkshire, in the nineteenth century, girls used turf for divination. A green bough, a bowl of water and a piece of turf were laid out and each girl, blindfolded, crawled towards them on hands and knees. To touch the turf first meant death, to touch the bough first meant widowhood. Right up to the end of the nineteenth century in Wales a sprinkling of earth was placed in coffins to help the souls of the departed find their way to the next world.

Holed stones have always been widely used as amulets and talismans, and could be of any size from small holed pebbles to huge monoliths. Most famous perhaps were those of the ancient ¬ivilisation of Babylonia where they were really on the grand scale, sculptured into enormous masses and wrought into the sides of buildings or placed in open spaces.

To counter evil spells or to cure simple ailments it was once thought to be enough to pass the body through a large holed stone, famous examples of which are the Crick, or Creeping Stone, at Madron, in Cornwall, the Shargar Stone of Fyvie, Aberdeenshire, and the menhirs of the Orkney Islands.

Superstitions and traditions often varied with the different localities where the holed stones were to be found. The smaller ones, called variously witch-stones, hag-stones, holy-stones, or mare-stones, were hung on doors and chimney breasts, round the necks of men and animals and over beds.

As John Aubrey, the antiquary, pointed out in his *Remaines of Gentilisme and Judaisme*, 'in the West of England (& I believe almost everywhere in this nation), the Carters, & Grooms, & Hostlers doe hang a flint (that has an hole in it) over horses that are hagge-ridden for a Preservative against it'. Thus holed-stones were hung in stables and byres to assist mares at foaling-time, to protect milk from witches and as a safeguard against a variety of possible misfortunes, natural and supernatural.

Lucky indeed was he who possessed a ring of amulet stones whether it be in the form of a necklace or bracelet, or somewhere about his domain. The ring most probably would have been made up of an Adder Stone, an Eagle Stone, an Irish Stone, a Logan Stone and a Toad Stone.

The Adder Stone, according to tradition, was generated by snakes, which, at certain times of the year, congregated in large colonies, coiled and emitted a saliva which hardened into stone. These were used to heal snake (particularly adder) bites, and in certain parts of Great Britain and Ireland, to cure whooping-cough and various eye troubles as well.

Eagle stones, actually *Lapis acquilaris*, were light brown aetites which were used to help women in labour and during pregnancy. Imported from the East, they were popular during the seventeenth and eighteenth centuries, and as many were expensive, a neighbourhood might share one for communal use in time of need. They were worn round the neck in a small bag by women during pregnancy and at the thigh during labour. The name was associated with an old belief that they could be found in eagles' nests, where the birds had placed them to ensure the fertility of their eggs.

Irish Stones were again mostly used to assist healing, and were especially efficacious if applied by an Irishman. Brought from Ireland, such stones were associated with St Patrick who is said to have used stones, blessed by his touch, to counter ill health. In the neighbourhood of Stamfordham, in England, there used to be three such stones and families brought their sick from miles around to touch them. Most stones of this type were unperforated.

Rocking Stones, or Logan Stones, were thought to be meeting-places of witches, either black or white. One stone, or boulder, placed on top of another qualified for this category, and anyone wishing to become a witch could do so by going to a Logan Stone at midnight and touching it the mystic nine times. Formerly, there was such a set of stones at Nancledra, near St Ives, to which children with rickets were brought at midnight to be rocked to normality. This cure, however, was claimed to work only for those born in wedlock!

Dark grey, or light brown stones were often called Toad Stones, and were for long alleged to come from the heads of old toads. Specially useful against sorcerers (they were reputed to change colour or sweat in the presence of evil), these stones were fashioned into rings or ornamental amulets. J. Lupton in his *A Thousand Notable Things* (1660) gives us a test for such a stone: 'holde the stone before a tode, so that he may see it; and if it be a right and true stone, the tode will leape towarde it, and make as though he would snatch it. He envieth so much that man should have that stone'.

A very common amulet, particularly worn for protection against cramp, was one made of cork, either as a pendant or a garter, and a cork held in the hand is still prescribed in some country districts as a sure relief from cramp. This ailment, too, was kept at bay, some said, with an amulet made of coffin nails, hinges, or handles, in which sextons used to do a flourishing trade. Rings made from coffin metal were thought to be specially curative if blessed by a reigning sovereign; from Edward the Confessor (1004–66) to the Reformation (sixteenth century) such rings were blessed on Good Friday, Queen Mary I being the last English ruler to perform the rite.

Stones again were believed by some actually to grow and multiply, and many an old-time farmer gave up trying to clear pebbly soil in the belief that as quickly as he might pick the pebbles out, they would become as profuse by the next day. Many parts of England fostered this belief, particularly Suffolk, where the larger pebbles were called Mother-stones, or Breeding-stones.

Amulets in the shape of glass walking-sticks, some filled with coloured sand, powder or hair, were hung up in houses to keep demons at bay. At night, any evil that might have come into a house, when the Devil rode in through the north window, would be attracted to the glass and could safely be wiped away after dawn. Instead of sand as filling many districts favoured beans, of which Molucca (or Virgin Mary) beans were particularly sought after in the Western Islands of Scotland. White beans were luckiest, but black ones were omens of death.

Another somewhat odd amulet, called a Life Token, was used to ascertain the well-being of an absent person by those left at home. A portion of the absent one's urine was kept in a container, securely corked. Should the liquid remain clear the absentee was well, but should it cloud danger or death was in store. Sometimes the tarnish on a knife left behind by a traveller was used as a similar indicator, both superstitions being particularly rife in earlier times when communications were poor.

The cult of horseshoe amulets and horsebrasses attained a wider popularity than most other charm objects, and the superstitions associated with them are numerous enough to fill a volume. Commonly believed to be lucky and used as a protective amulet, the horseshoe has obvious connections with the mystic powers of iron and fire. Finding horseshoes was considered particularly lucky and in some districts a correct procedure was laid down for the finder, like this Shropshire advice:

> Pick'en up 'e 'orse's shoe, and spatter en wi' spittle.
> Mak' a wish fully quickly and throw en o'er't shoother
> (shoulder), walk on by an' ne'er glance'e back.

The usual practice, of course, was to pick up the horseshoe and take it home to nail on the front door, or over a threshold, or, as Admiral Lord Nelson did, to the mainmast of your ship. Care had to be taken, however, to ensure that the points of the shoe were uppermost, else the good luck would drain away.

Superstitions often mix Christianity and pagan practice, as in this charm to be incanted while the horseshoe is being nailed to the door:

> Father, Son and Holy Ghost,
> Nail the devil to this post,
> Thrice I smites with Holy Crook,
> With this mell I thrice do knock,
> One for God,
> > And one for Wod(en)
> > And one for Lok(i).

Elegant horsebrasses, once the pride and joy of many carters, were originally more than mere ornaments. They were really intended as amulets to protect horses from the ubiquitous Evil Eye, horses having always been believed to be particularly vulnerable to the influence of witches and fairies.

21

Examples from Mycenae, dated around 3500 BC, show how very old is the cult of decorating animals with talismans for their protection. In ancient Egypt, too, 1,300 years ago, dogs and cats were ornamented with amulets of the god Utchat.

Shiny metal was generally preferred for these early decorations, on the grounds that its dazzling effect could best be relied upon to deflect the Evil Eye. And belief in the power of the Evil Eye was strong right up to the beginning of the twentieth century, when Neapolitan cab-drivers were still decorating their horses with mystic protective symbols.

The circle symbol was the simplest form of all and had certain connections with deities like, Io, daughter of the river god Inachus, Diana, goddess of the hunt, or Isis (Hathor), a goddess depicted in the form of a cow.

Decorative brasses date from around Assyrian times, say AD 650, with the disc again predominating. Similar examples have been found in the Six Dynasties (AD 221–589) in China, the corresponding eras in Japan, tenth-century India and first-century Norway.

In Britain, there is direct evidence of horses being decorated at least from the Iron Age, and of later fashions being dictated by Roman influence and by souvenirs brought home by the Crusaders.

The positions for brasses on a horse were as follows: on the fly terret (or swinger) at the top of the head-piece, the brow band, the face piece (or flash), the blinker, the nose band, the collar, the martingale (with sets of brasses, five or under), the belly-band, or girth, the breeching, the crupper, the saddle, the flyer, or saddle centre-piece, and the hame-piece. Sometimes the hame-piece had a little set of bells attached, a survival of the old latten bells, with inscriptions of loyalty to the royal house, or a set of Prince of Wales feathers.

Popular shapes were animals, birds, heraldic devices, fabulous beasts, acorns, hearts, flowers, swastikas, commemorative plates and society and trade emblems, all with their mystic associations. Really old horsebrasses are of considerable value and modern reproductions are widely bought nowadays as house decorations.

Talismans have been variously inscribed on swords, crowns, cups, drums, trumpets, roods and banners, stones, stocks and gems. Sometimes it was thought necessary to authenticate a talisman so that there could be no doubt of its powers. An example is the Sacred Lance of the Holy Roman Emperors, known as the Spear of St Maurice, which incorporates crosses supposedly made by one of the nails from the True Cross. The inscription reads:

> CLAVVS DOMINICUS X HEINRICVS D:I:GRA TERCIIS
> ROMANO IMPERATOR AUG HOC ARGENTVM JUSSIT
> FABRICARI AD CONFIRMATIONE DNI ET LANCEE
> SANCTI MAVRICCI: SANCTVS MAVRICVS.

> (The Nail of Our Lord X Henry by the Grace of God the third of the Roman Emperor Augustus, ordered this (plate of) silver to be made for proof of the Nail of Our Lord and the Lance of St Maurice. St Maurice.)

Those who made amulets and talismans in former times were either greatly venerated or mortally feared for their supposed powers, and in Scotland in particular the use and manufacture of such objects was a capital crime. In 1678 Sir George Mackenzie of Rosehaugh, King's Advocate, tried to justify this barbarity:

> Though charms be not able to produce the effects that are punishable in witches, yet since these effects cannot be produced without the devil, and (since) he will not employ himself at the desire of any who have not resigned themselves wholly to him, it is very just that the users of these should be punished, being guilty at least of apostasy and heresy.

Like attitudes continued for many years, but none the less sales of amulets against evil retribution showed a marked increase after most witch trials.

People like Robert Herrick (1591–1674), the poet, however, continued to poke fun at the foolish and the pompous:

> Holy water come and bring,
> Cast in salt for seasoning,
> Set the brush for sprinkling;
> Sacred spittle bring ye hither,
> Meal and it now mix together,
> And a little oil to either.
> Give the tapers here their light.
> Ring the saints' bell to affright
> Far from hence the evil sprite.

Superstitions concerning the supposed magic powers of money stems mostly from religio-folk ideas. Sacrament Money, that offered at Holy Communion, was taken to have curative powers and to be of particular use in the healing of epilepsy and rheumatism. According to custom, twelve or thirteen pieces of coin were collected by friends of a sick person and exchanged for a coin of larger denomination which came from the Communion offertory. This coin was then beaten by a blacksmith, the usual medium between pagan and religious country rites, and worn by the sick person round the neck on a ribbon. At West Bromwich, in Staffordshire, until late into the 1890s, rheumatism was regularly treated by rubbing such an amulet on the affected part.

Certain magic coins, too, have for long been associated with a district or family. The famous Black Penny, for instance, belonged to the Turnbull family of Hume-Byers, in Northumberland, and was used as an amulet against madness in animals. Frequently borrowed even by farmers in Yorkshire and Durham, the coin had to be dipped in a south-running stream or river, and a quantity of this potent water was then fed to the sick animal. In the tracts of M. A. Denham, the following is stated about the penny, which seems to have been lost around 1827:

> (it was) not quite so large as a common penny, but thicker. It had a kind of raised rim or border, and seemed to be composed of copper and zinc. It had been in the (Turnbull) family for a hundred years at least . . . once a purse containing gold . . . was left as a deposit for its safe return.

A similar penny, or at least a fairly large piece of silver, belonging to a Scottish family at Lockerby, in Dumfriesshire, was also lent out to farmers for the cure of hydrophobia and madness in cattle. The penny was dipped in water which was then stirred vigorously with a cleft stick, the resultant magic brew being fed to the cattle. People bought bottled 'Lockerby Water' as a patent medicine, and in the *Gateshead Observer* of 23 March 1844 it is recorded, 'a large supply (of the water was) procured by voluntary subscription'.

Professor Sir James Y. Simpson (1811–70), discoverer of the use of chloroform as an anaesthetic, at a meeting of the Scottish Society of Antiquaries on 8 April 1861, read a paper on the superstitions concerning Scottish magic charm stones, and in it noted: 'In the present century this ancient medical charm stone has acquired a worldwide reputation as the original *Talisman* of Sir Walter Scott, though latterly its therapeutic reputation has greatly declined, and almost ceased.'

He was, of course, referring to the famous Lee Penny, a small, triangular, dark red stone, set into the reverse side of an Edward I groat (a silver coin worth about 4d). It was said to have been in the possession of the Lockhart family of Lee Castle, in north-west Lanarkshire; one, Sir Simon Lockhart, having brought it back from the Holy Land. The penny was thought to have been able to cure rabies, haemorrhage and sundry cattle ailments, and on one occasion the people of Newcastle borrowed the penny, against a bond of £6,000, to arrest a plague.

A later member of the family, Sir James Lockhart, found the heirloom something of an embarrassment when, on 21 October 1638, he was arraigned before the Synod of Glasgow for the use of the penny in witchcraft. At that trial was Robert Young, the Assembly Clerk, who left this record:

> Quhilk day, amongst the referries of the Brethren of the Ministry of Lanark, it was proposed to the Synod that Gavin Hamilton of Raploch had pursueit an Complaint before them against Sir James Lockhart of Lee, anent the superstitious using of an Stone set in silver, for the curing of deseased Cattle, qlk the said Gavin affirmed could not be lawfully usit, and that they had deferrit to give ony decisionne thairin till the advice of the Assemblie might be had concerning the same. The Assemblie having inquirit of the manner of using thereof, and particularly understood, be examination of the said Laird of Lee and otherwise, that the custom is only to cast the stone in some water and give the deseasit cattle thereof to drink, and that the same is done without using any words, such as Charmers and Sorcereirs use in thair unlawfull practices; and considering that in nature thair are many things seen to work strange effects, whereof no human wit can give a reason, it having pleased God to give to stones and herbs a speciall vertue for healing of many infirmities in man and beast, advises the Brethren to surcease thair process, as therein they perceive no ground of Offence, and admonishes the said Laird of Lee, in the using of the said stone, to take heid that it be usit hereafter with the least scandle that possibly maybe.

Special coins, called 'touch pieces', were minted and distributed extensively in England at 'healing by touch' ceremonies, especially for scrofula (King's Evil), a disease marked by chronic swellings of the glands in various parts of the body, particularly the neck, which tended to suppurate. According to

26

both Tacitus (*History*, IV, lxxxi) and Seutonius (*Vespasian*, VII), the Emperor Vespasian effected miraculous cures at Alexandria with his touch. Edward the Confessor is the first English king on record, in 1058, to 'touch' for scrofula.

Tudor and Stuart monarchs used the gold angel in touching, the coin symbolically showing St Michael's defeat of the Devil. Many of these coins were punched for suspension round the neck or over a diseased member. Charles II medalets bore the inscription *Soli dea gloria* (To God alone be the Glory), while Edward III gold coins bore legends such as, 'But Jesus, passing through the midst of them, went his way.' Such coins were also used to ward off thieves.

James Edward Stuart, the Old Pretender, claimed regal healing powers, as did his sons. Eventually, the practice was repudiated by William III and finally abandoned by George I. So strong was the superstition attaching to these coins that Queen Anne touched Samuel Johnson at the age of two and a half for scrofula; the medal she gave him was much revered and is now to be seen in the British Museum.

Amulet coins were also common in China and Korea and, at times, current coins made from melted-down images of Buddha, fetched more than their face value when sold as amulets.

Many Chinese, Korean and Japanese coins have little marks on their reverses which resemble nail-marks. It is said that a Chinese empress accidentally left her nail-marks on a clay coin mould and, because her touch was considered celestial and the mark likely to bring good luck, it was retained and subsequently imitated on many other coins. In China, too, a clay fish was often used as 'spirit money', and one called a *yei pi* was found in a tomb beside the Yellow River in Honan dating from *circa* 1122–255 BC.

The use of amulets and talismans as jewellery dates, as we have seen, from very early times. Czars and princes, kings and bishops, movie stars and tycoons have all relied upon 'lucky' charms and various types of jewelled amulets. The centre-stone of each piece has usually been dictated by the month of the wearer's birth, as in the following, or some similar system:

Garnet (red, sometimes brown, green, yellow and black; green was considered an unlucky colour for all those not born in May; brown stood for fading affection), JANUARY for truth and constancy.

Amethyst (bluish-violet, a grave colour but useful in restoring health to the sick), FEBRUARY, denoted sincerity, and helped to keep the wearer sober.

Bloodstone (dark-green variegated with red jasper), MARCH, for courage and presence of mind.

Diamond, APRIL, for innocence and light.

Emerald, MAY, for love potency.

Pearl, or *Agate,* JUNE, the latter denoting health and long life and a counter against poison, while the pearl stood for purity and tears.

Ruby (Carnelian), JULY, contentment, courage.

Sardonyx (reddish), AUGUST, for married bliss.

Sapphire, SEPTEMBER, the magic stone of Jupiter, an antidote for misery.

Opal, OCTOBER, stood for hope, but unlucky for those not born in this month.

Topaz, NOVEMBER, fidelity.

Turquoise, DECEMBER, prosperity.

But certain stones have proved to be disastrous for some; and diamonds have been singled out as the most likely to attract evil and the most dangerous to girls.

One well-known diamond, believed to have been ripped from the forehead of an Indian idol by a wandering French mendicant, brought death and ill-fortune to most of its successive owners. Said to have come into the possession of King Louis XIV of France, who gave it to his mistress, Mme de Montespan, legend traces the 44½-carat stone through the hands of the unfortunate Marie Antoinette, executed in 1793, to one Henry Thomas Hope, an English banker who bought the stone in 1830.

Thereafter the Hope family fell on evil times, and subsequent owners who also met with tragedy or misfortune included Jacques Colet (suicide), Prince Ivan Kanitovitsky (murdered), Sultan Abdul Hamed of Turkey (dethroned), Simon Montharides (he and his family were killed by a shying horse) and a number of others.

Around 1907 an American, Evalyn Walsh McLean, bought the stone for £8,000 (then about $40,000), following which Mrs McLean lost a son, a daughter and her husband in tragic circumstances. Her heir, Miss Evalyn McLean, too, was found dead at Dallas, Texas, in mysterious circumstances on 13 December 1967.

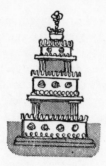

3

Of Wedding Bells and Baby Charms

In marrying psychiatrist Andrea Dotti at the same place, Morges, in Switzerland, where she had married and divorced her first husband, Mel Ferrer, film star Audrey Hepburn disregarded the superstition that to marry twice in the same place brought certain bad luck.

Time, place and season have always dictated certain courses of action to the superstitious, May in particular being a month to avoid for marriage. When the ill-fated Mary, Queen of Scots, married James Hepburn, Earl of Bothwell, on 15 May 1567, one person made his views quite clear by penning the line '*mense malas maio nubere vulgus ait*,' from Publius Ovidius Naso, on the gates of Holyrood Palace, Edinburgh. The tag has passed into folk doggerel as:

> The people say
> That only wantons marry
> In the month of May.

Although this month seems to have been shunned for marriage since Roman times, with Plutarch pointing out that it was the month when the spirits of the dead were honoured, the superstition is probably older than that; the ancient *Sarum Missal* proves the English Christian avoidance of this month.

Superstitions about marriage did, however, sometimes conflict and while folk in Yorkshire avoided 21 December (St Thomas's Day) for weddings, those of the neighbouring county of Lincolnshire thought the day most auspicious. Again, in East Anglia, 15 July (St Swithin's Day) was avoided for weddings, while in northern regions it was considered a particularly lucky day.

During past centuries Acts of Parliament and canons of the Church have prohibited marriage during certain months, as the *Almanac Galen* of 1642 records:

> Times prohibiting marriage this year:
> From the 27 November till January 13,
> From Februarie 6 untill April 18,
> From May 16 untill June 6.

And from the register of St Mary's, Beverley, in Yorkshire, for 1641:

> When Advent comes do thou refraine,
> Till Hillary set ye free againe;
> Next Septuagesima saith thee nay,
> But when Lowe Sunday comes thou may;
> But at Rogation thou must tarry,
> Till Trinitie shall bid thee marry.

Weekdays have been variously assessed:

> Monday for wealth—lucky in most parts
> Tuesday for health—lucky in most parts

Wednesday the best day of all—especially in the English Midlands

Thursdays for losses—particularly in Britain, Holland
and Switzerland, but good in Shropshire

Fridays for crosses—bad for Christians, but good for
Norsemen

And Saturday no luck at all—most popular day of all
in modern times

Concerning weather on the wedding day, superstitions are
equally conflicting, and the general belief that 'Happy is the
bride the sun shines on', becomes, in Hampshire, Derbyshire
and Lincolnshire, 'Lucky the bride the rain rains on'.

Long before her wedding day, however, a girl's life path was
crossed by superstition. Great care had to be taken in the choice
of the correct engagement-ring stone, and every precaution
taken against losing the ring (foretelling an ending) or dam-
aging it (death or desertion). A girl could also do much to help
herself find a likely spouse or to win the man of her choice.

Girls from Texas carried toads around to attract love, while
their Balkan sisters collected earth which a handsome man had
walked upon; this earth they put with a bulb into a pot, and if
a flower subsequently bloomed the man would love the planter
alone.

In Germany, a herb was used for divination, as this old poem
shows:

> The young maid stole from the cottage door,
> And blushed as she sought the plant of power.
> 'Thou silver glow-worm, oh, lend me thy light,
> I must gather the mystic St John's wort tonight—
> The wonderful herb whose leaf shall decide
> If the coming year shall make me a bride'.

While Clare wrote thus in his *Calendar*:

> Or, trying simple charms and spells,
> Which rural superstitions tells,

32

They pull the little blossom threads
From out the knotwood's button heads.
Then, if they guess aright, the swain
Their love's sweet fancies try to gain,
'Tis said that ere it lies an hour,
'Twill blossom with a second flower.

Some took even more drastic measures; in Ireland a boy would steal a hair from the head of the beloved, thread it on a needle, dig up a corpse, and pass the needle through the arm of the cadaver, thus making himself irresistible to the girl!

In Italy, girls would utter this after evening devotions just before leaving church:

I take not oil for my affliction
But take I the benediction.
From the hand of Saint Maria
To move the man to me so dear.
Mother may he ne'er depart
The safety of my tender heart.

A girl in many parts of the USA, however, relied upon a wink at the brightest star she could see before going to bed.

Love potions are as old as love itself and from classical times herbs and exotic ingredients have been used as cures, poisons and aphrodisiacs. And although this practice was not peculiar to witches, those who made up such concoctions were usually branded as such.

At one time it used to be considered unlucky for a betrothed couple to hear their own banns read in church; to do so was to risk evil shadows being cast across their future children in the form of dumbness or idiocy. And to break off the engagement after the final reading of the banns was really courting misfortune. It could also render the young couple liable to a fine, a form of retribution which was regularly meted out at several towns in Norfolk.

33

Couples who lived together in defiance of the Church were burnt in effigy to appease the Devil, or were kept awake at night by a cacophony of village drums, horns, trumpets and cymbal crashing outside their homes. Such punishment could be meted out to whole villages who erred *en masse*, and was the usual course of action when common people could not obtain satisfaction from the Law. Instead, they dispensed their own justice in the form of noisy shamanistic dances to drive away devils.

Wedding cakes, dresses and veils also attracted superstitions. A very ancient feature of the marriage feast, the wedding cake symbolised fertility and good luck, which could be especially encouraged if one was thrown at the bride! In Yorkshire, it used to be the custom for a plate of wedding cake to be thrown from the upper window of the bride's house on her return from church, to ensure for her a happy marriage.

In Roman society, the bride and groom as well as the guests had the cake of *confarreation* crumbled over their heads to ensure plentifulness. About the same time in Macedonia, families prepared elaborate cakes for luck the Monday before the wedding day. The bride was expected to knead the mixture herself while a boy stood near her long bowl with a ceremonial sword raised ready to drive away demons, which might try to get into the cake. When the mixture was finished, a ring and a coin were thrown in, and whoever found the ring could demand a ransom from the groom.

At Anglo-Saxon weddings, large baskets of cakes were prepared for distribution to guests. Each visitor was given one for luck by the bride's family and probably kept it for a while to enjoy the benefits. In China, it was the groom who gave the cakes away for luck. A later English custom was for each guest to bring his own cake, or spiced bun, which were piled into a large mound. The bride and groom had then to attempt to kiss each other over the pile without knocking any off. If they were successful, lifelong prosperity was assured. And one of the oldest superstitions, still prevalent today, is that any unmarried girl who sleeps with a piece of bridal cake under her pillow will dream of her future husband.

Prosperity and fecundity could be baked into a wedding cake, or so this Elizabethan rhyme suggests:

> Today, my Julia, thee must make,
> For mistresse bride an weddinge cake;
> Kneade but the dow, and it wille be,
> Turned to prosperitie by thee.
> Now the paste of almonds fine,
> Assures a broode o' childer nine.

The Iroquois Indians of the USA, too, believed that cake at a wedding brought good luck; each cake was first inspected for demons by the witch-doctor, who then anointed them for the bride to present to the groom. In Fiji and some other primitive cultures the public eating of a cake could alone constitute a marriage ceremony.

The custom of leaping soon after the wedding ceremony is old in origin and sometimes special barriers were erected outside the church for the couple to jump over. Within living memory 'barring the way' was a common custom. Sometimes the bridegroom was expected to pay to pass out of the church-yard; villagers gathered with chains and ropes to impede his path. At Eyemouth in Scotland, in 1953, a bridal pair were hemmed in with fishermen's creels and rope until the groom gave money to the creelmen.

Because she was entering into an entirely new life, every item of a bride's trousseau had to be new, except, of course, for the customary 'something old, something borrowed and something blue'. Brides were also warned about the dangers of making their own dresses; to do this would attract misfortune. Furthermore no bride should be completely attired before the actual ceremony, and sometimes a glove button was left unfastened until the bride reached the altar.

35

Colours too had to be watched:

> Blue for a bride and she will rue
> But dressed in white her lover's true.
> Yellow's by the saints forsworn
> And purple makes a bride aye morn.
> Nothing green for a fine day,
> But pink for the darling buds of May.

And the curious:

> Oxford lasses shun the brown
> For they can never live in town.

Colours and superstitions also applied to a bride's veil, a garment used for divination in Nottingham. These sempstresses were wont to gather up to the middle of the last century while one of their number was selected as the diviner. A hair was then taken from the head of the fairest girl and worked into a bride's veil to assure a long and happy married life. If, at the beginning of the process, the hair should break, the bride's early death was foretold; a break at the end prophesied a similar fate for her husband.

In some places, to take off a wedding ring once it had been placed on in church was believed to be courting disaster; but this is by no means a general superstition and borrowed wedding rings have long been used in folk-cures and for divination. But to drop the ring before the ceremony has always been considered disastrous, a sign of the premature death of whichever partner dropped it.

Straw, long associated with fertility rites, was at one time made into a garter in Yorkshire for a bride to wear to assure fecundity (as was a garter or bangle of shells). For male babies, wheaten straw was sought, and oat straw for female. After the straw had been placed around the girl's thigh, she sang a special Straw Song, or recited any passage from the Bible which referred to straw, as in the account of the manger at Bethlehem.

Only a virgin could wear such a garter, lapsed virtue was held to attract evil.

These days it is considered unlucky for the bride and groom to see each other on their wedding day, before they actually meet in church. In past times, some rural communities favoured 'walking weddings' in which the couple walked in the same procession to and from the church, the bride being careful to leave home by the front door, placing her right foot over the threshold first. Were the bride to meet a pig, or a funeral, these were considered bad omens indeed, but lucky if she met a black cat, a chimney-sweep or an elephant! Grey horses were prescribed for the carriage, but should they refuse to start before or after the ceremony bad luck was in store.

Many of the churches of rural England had what was known as a lychgate, or corpse gate, 'lych' being the old English word for a dead body. At this gate a priest would first meet a funeral procession and begin the service while the coffin rested on a wooden or stone bench. Few lychgates of a date earlier than the seventeenth century (some have been restored and rebuilt) exist today, but some of the old superstitions associated with them still persist. One very old belief of bad luck was for a bridal procession to have to pass through a lychgate on the way to church, and at Kneesall Church, in Nottinghamshire, two entrances were made, one for corpses and the other for brides.

At Fingest, in Buckinghamshire, a special ceremony took place at the church gate:

> No wedding at Fingest is supposed to be lucky unless the bridegroom lifts his bride over the church gate when leaving after the ceremony. The gate is locked so that the newly-wedded couple cannot get through it, while all their relations and friends gather to watch the custom being duly observed. (*Fingest Church Guide Book,* 1956.)

No bridal procession ever passes over the bridge at Hoxne in Suffolk. For here it was, according to local legend, that

Edmund, saint and martyr, hid on his flight from the Danes. A newly-married couple saw him and gave his position away to his foes. As he died, Edmund laid a curse on every couple who should cross the bridge on their wedding day.

Confetti is the last remaining trace of an old pagan fertility rite. It symbolises the corn that was used in ancient times to ensure prosperity and faithfulness in marriage. In north Nottinghamshire and in Sussex, ears of wheat were thrown instead.

Until as late as the 1850s, in many districts a husband was responsible for his wife's pre-marital debts; from this grew the legend that a husband would not be liable for any such debts if the wife were wed naked save for a shift or smock, and such 'smock' weddings have been recorded in Cumberland, Yorkshire and Lincolnshire. It was also believed that the obvious poverty of the bride would discourage the attention of greedy demons.

Most counties in Great Britain had their own favourite superstitions about marriage; here are a few:

North Lancashire: Let a girl hang a wishbone over the door on New Year's Day and the first man who enters will become her husband.

Cumberland: Three candles burning in one room signify that there will soon be a wedding in the house.

Kirkcudbrightshire, Scotland: No wedding in a house while peacock's feathers are displayed.

Cheshire: A girl who builds-up a bright fire quickly will make a good wife.

Fife, Scotland: If a bride eats a cake of sugar on her wedding day, her husband will be as loving after the wedding as he was before it.

Pregnancy was looked upon in the past as an extremely hazardous time, not only because of the dangers of the actual delivery, but also because of the evil spirits who were believed to surround women at that time. In some primitive civilisations women were even expected to retire into complete seclusion until after the birth, in case the aura of spirits around them contaminated others.

Within living memory a pregnant woman's touch was thought pernicious, and she was debarred from all household duties and kept well away from flowers, foodstuffs and livestock. Similar superstitions were attached to menstruation and both in Japan and among certain North American tribes women and girls were put into purdah at these times.

Superstitions about dangers to an unborn child have always abounded. In Wales, it was thought that should a pregnant woman spin during gestation her baby would ultimately die by hanging. Again, should she step over a grave, her baby would surely die prematurely.

Another belief, that if a pregnant woman met a hare her baby would have a hare-lip, was based on the notion that a hare was a common form for a witch to take. In his *Daemonologie* (1650), Nathaniel Hone records that on meeting a hare 'some in companie with a woman greate with childe (did) cut or (tear) some of the clothes off that woman with childe, to prevent the ill luck that might befall her'.

Before the advent of modern obstetrics many strange things were done to assist birth. Special witch-proof nails were driven into beds, charm objects were arranged in the delivery room and dry earth was sprinkled on a floor so that the woman giving birth might draw strength at her climax. Again, all doors in the house were opened and all knots untied to assist an easy delivery. For many years, too, the use of anaesthetics to relieve birth pangs was considered an interference with the intentions of God. Queen Victoria helped to break this superstition by being one of the first to allow herself be anaesthetised during a birth. If born by Caesarian operation, a child was supposed to have unusual strength, to be able to see spirits, and even to locate buried treasure.

One of the oldest of human superstitions, the cause of birthmarks, is said to derive from a woman having been 'touched by some malignante bodie' during pregnancy. A folk-cure practised in the home counties of England, up to the 1950s, was regular massage of the birthmarks with saliva, preferably from a donor who had been through a period of fasting.

In *David Copperfield*, Charles Dickens notes in his opening chapter the efficacy against drowning of a caul, a thin membrane over the head with which some babies are born. Sailors often bought these as charms against shipwreck, and in Scotland a caul gave protection against the Evil Eye, as well as bestowing second sight. In Holland, it was thought to have given power to see ghosts. During the early 1800s cauls fetched as much as £20 ($48) each, although David Copperfield's only brought five shillings from an old lady 'all in halfpence, and twopence halfpenny short. . . . It is a fact which will be long remembered as remarkable . . . that she was never drowned, but died triumphantly in bed, at ninety-two'.

While a child born with a caul was supposed also to have the gifts of an orator, the posthumous child—one whose mother did not survive its birth—was deemed to have healing powers. Even today instances still occur of posthumous children being called in to cure thrush, whooping-cough and respiratory ailments by breathing the 'kiss-of-life' into the sick. Likewise a 'footling', a child born feet first, was called upon to help heal those suffering from lumbago, rheumatism and muscular pain.

Superstitious folk in Illinois have always held that a baby born with a double-crown marking on its head (the shape of the lines of the parietal and coronal suture bones) would live on two continents, while in Massachusetts such markings were said to mean that the baby would break bread in two countries. In Georgia, a child was believed to acquire a similar nature and disposition to those of the person who first carried him out of doors.

Between birth and baptism a child was thought to be highly susceptible to the machinations of the Prince of Darkness. In

Cumberland, a baby's head was washed with rum to drive away evil spirits, while in Wales honey was prescribed for the same purpose. Various protective charms, too, were given to a baby, such as eggs, salt, matchboxes, or even a sixpence, while in East Anglia a virgin's kisses were thought the most beneficial of all.

Unbaptised babies were considered likely to have more ailments than baptised ones and, if they died, would certainly not be admitted into Heaven. After death, the folk in Yorkshire said, the unbaptised spirit lived as a nightjar or, in Devon, became one of the Yeth Hounds which hunted on Dartmoor with the Devil.

In Oxfordshire, in particular, it was thought unlucky to weigh a baby until it was twelve months old and, at Bedford, people were warned against stepping over a crawling child in case they stunted its growth.

A belief still very much alive in Britain is that a woman's first steps outside her house after a birth should be to church; to ignore the ritual was considered to be inviting misfortune, while in parts of Northumberland and Durham she was thought to be putting herself outside protection of the law. The 'churching' of women after childbirth is, of course, an age-old religious practice but along the borders of Wales it was long considered unlucky for a husband to attend his wife's churching.

A curious superstition still practised in primitive societies is the 'couvade', when a husband retires to bed, or to the family hut, with sympathy labour pains when his wife is about to be delivered. In Yorkshire, when a girl who had had an illegitimate child would not reveal the father's name, a search was made in the neighbourhood for any man ill in bed; such a coincidence of illness was taken as proof of paternity. Among the Basques, and in Corsica, the father of the baby was pampered and propped up in bed with the child by his side while his wife, who had just had the baby, was sent out to work! The object of the couvade was certainly protection against evil and often a man pretended to have the labour pains to confuse any malignant spirits who might have designs on the child in his wife's womb.

'If you rock an empty cradle, it will soon be filled,' they said in Huntingdonshire, but in the Scottish Border country, and in Cornwall, it was considered unlucky to do so, and downright dangerous between birth and baptism.

Holy Innocents' Day, 28 December (formerly called Childermass Day) was thought to be the unluckiest day of the year. For then it was that Herod, the tyrannical King of Judea, ordered the massacre of the children.

King Edward IV's coronation was postponed because the day first chosen coincided with Childermass, and King Louis XI of France refused to contract any business on that day. In Britain, up to the early 1900s, all new building and travelling was put off if Childermass was near, but in Lancashire it was thought a good day for children's parties.

Gregory, in his *Episcopus Puerorum in Die Innocentium* (1684), records that at the end of Childermass, children were superstitiously and ceremonially beaten, 'that the memorie of this murther might stick the closer; and, in a moderate proportion, to act over the crueltie again in kind'.

A number of superstitions similar to those associated with baptism also surrounded the confirmation ceremony and there is the classic case of one old woman in Hertfordshire who was confirmed no less than three times as a cure for rheumatism.

4

The Magic of Numbers

The superstition of numbers is perhaps one of the most curious of all. Since the time of Pythagoras (*circa* 582–507 BC), the most influential of the early Greek scientists, numbers and their multiples have been deemed by the common man to have occult significance, particularly odd numbers; although the ancient priests of Egypt were using numbers in their divination for five thousand years before that. The lowest numbers were deemed to be the most potent, as anything over ten would have some mystic relation to the numbers making them up; ie 21 would have the secret overtones of 1 and 2, as well as the two combined. A legacy of this mysticism was the reluctance of people in many rural areas to divulge their ages, in case the numbers could somehow be used to invoke evil upon them.

For centuries people have gone to infinite trouble to work out 'systems' of divination to discover good-luck dates and number

43

sequences for their advantage. Among such systems were those giving letters of the alphabet corresponding numbers:

1	2	3	4	5	6	7	8	9
A	B	C	D	E	F	G	H	I
J	K	L	M	N	O	P	Q	R
S	T	U	V	W	X	Y	Z	

and using these to work out personal numbers. Thus, using this system, someone called JOHN SMITH would have a birth number of:

J	O	H	N		S	M	I	T	H
1	6	8	5		1	4	9	2	8

which added: $= 1 + 6 + 8 + 5 + 1 + 4 + 9 + 2 + 8 = 44$, reduced again $(4 + 4)$ to a single number 8. This number would then be considered to have a mystic influence on all events in John Smith's life.

Again birthdays were sometimes used. Suppose a person's date of birth was 20 September 1939. Reduced to numbers, this equals: $20 + 9$ (the number of the month) $+ 1939 =$ (discarding the noughts) $2 + 9 + 1 + 9 + 3 + 9 = 33 =$ $(3 + 3$, as above$) = 6$. Or, arriving at the same number by another method:

Day number   20
Month number $9 = 1968 = 24 = 6$
Year numbers   1939

Man began to count at an early date on one hand, usually the right. The Romans utilised this in their number system: I finger, II fingers, III fingers, IIII fingers, IIIII fingers; the latter number however soon came to represent the hand and thus was written as 'V' for an open hand (the Greek word for 'count' really means 'five').

Over the years, the numbers acquired occult significance.

I (1)—Indivisible, but with the overtones of death and dissolution, this number is given a male aura, the symbol of God, the Creator of Life; or to pagans, the symbol of a phallus. A person with a birth number of one is considered happy-go-lucky; and a house with this number is reputed to have thriftless occupants.

II (2)—Given a female aura, this number is dedicated to love and the coming together of two kindred spirits. A house numbered two is supposed to have truculent tenants.

III (3)—Strangely enough, both pagan and Christian societies looked upon this number as béing lucky; to the Christians it signified the Trinity. But luck, or ill-fortune, seems to have been governed in ancient times by threefold aspects. In many country parishes, deaths were expected to occur in threes; and it is a general belief that accidents, receipt of gifts, letters and so on are liable to occur in threes, thus mirroring the religious triads of the Three Fates and the Three Graces. Many old charms were repeated three times for potency, success with money was forecast for those living in a house numbered three, while in the East, the third day of the new moon is the most fortunate day in a month.

IV (4)—Was the numeral sacred to the Pythagoreans, representing Endurance, Discovery and Completeness. Encompassing the four elements, Air, Earth, Fire and Water, four is perhaps the luckiest of the even numbers in superstition. Not so, however, in Japan, where the numeral *yon* is usually substituted for the Chinese-derived *shi* (four) because of its similarity to the sound of *shi* (death).

V (5)—Originally denoting the end of all things, five was a number magically used by the Greeks and Romans. Christians usually associate five with the five wounds of Christ; but there are a number of variants (five books of Moses, and so on).

VI (6)—An unlucky number for those who are dishonest. Although universally a doubtful number, those with the birth number of six were thought likely to attain fame and skill in prophecy. The triad of six, 6 + 6 + 6, is the mystic number spoken of in the Apocalypse (the name of the last book of the

New Testament). Perhaps the best solution of the riddle is *Neron Kesar,* the Hebrew form of the Latin, Nero, Caesar. Expressing this, removing the 'a' and 'e' as in the ancient Hebrew writing practice, we have: NERON KESAR.

N R O N K S R
$50 + 200 + 6 + 50 + 100 + 60 + 200 = 666$

which may be resolved to 6 again: $6 + 6 + 6 = 18 (1 + 8)$ $= 9 (3 + 3) = 6$. At one time the significance of this was a dangerous secret, the potency of which has been lost to us in modern times.

VII (7)—A wonderful number for most people, and sacred to the Persians, Assyrians, Chaldeans and the Hebrews. The Goths had seven gods and, according to astrologers, man's years were divided into seven parts ruled by seven planets:

> Infancy of four years governed by Moon
> Childhood of ten years governed by Mercury
> Youth of eight years governed by Venus
> Adolescence of twenty years governed by Sun
> Manhood of fourteen governed by Mars
> Old Age of twelve years governed by Jupiter
> Decrepitude of two years governed by Saturn
> making seventy years in all.

Mentioned over three hundred times in the Bible, the number seven was considered lucky by Adolf Hitler who mounted his major attacks (Russia, Poland, Netherlands, Austria, Greece, Yugoslavia) on this day.

VIII (8)—Considered a characterless number sometimes pointing to survival (eight people were preserved on the Ark during the Flood).

IX (9)—As a multiple of three, nine is usually believed to be lucky. The Anglo-Saxons used this number in healing and spell-breaking.

X (10)—Not much can be said about this number except that it has Christian overtones (the Ten Commandments).

XI (11)—Usually considered an unlucky number, but for no apparent reason.

XII (12)—Some point to the fact that there were twelve apostles (or twelve sons of Jacob, tribes of Israel, or months of the year) as evidence for associating good luck with this number.

XIII (13)—Most people believe this number to be unlucky and some have even developed an allergy to it—known as 'triskaidekaphobia'. Once used as a vague number for anything over twelve, thirteen was a death sign for the Romans, and presaged disaster to the Christians (thirteen at the Last Supper). Curiously enough, thirteen people were present when Loki, the red-haired Norse evil-doer, killed the handsome Baldur, favourite of the gods. Thus thirteen passed into Norse mythology as an unlucky number. Ignoring possible bad luck, the Seal of the President of the United States incorporates eight groups of thirteen stars to represent the original thirteen states. Many communities, however, look upon the number as lucky, particularly those who live in towns or cities whose names contain thirteen letters.

Finally, an odd significance of the number 'twenty' for Presidents of the United States of America, all of whom, elected at intervals of twenty years from 1840, *have died in office*:

1840	William Henry Harrison
1860	Abraham Lincoln
1880	James A. Garfield
1900	William McKinley
1920	Warren G. Harding
1940	Franklin D. Roosevelt
1960	John F. Kennedy

Small wonder if superstitious candidates at the Presidential elections in 1980 feel a trifle uneasy!

5

Sacred Trees and Favoured Flora

Even before man had emerged from the cave-dwelling era, he looked upon trees as the abodes of supernatural beings of infinite powers for good or evil. And as most of those forces were evil, he would choose for his home a site where trees were either absent or of friendly influence.

Curiously enough he regarded the blackthorn, with its white blossom and black branches, as evil and avoided it as an omen; curiously, because with the advent of Christianity the blackthorn from which Christ's crown of thorns was believed to have been made, was again abhorred and never brought indoors.

The people of Worcestershire, however, took a different view and on New Year's morning, just before dawn, a crown of blackthorn would be made and baked in an oven until calcined. This ash was then taken to a cornfield and scattered to ensure a plentiful crop. In Herefordshire, scorched blackthorn was mixed with mistletoe as a Christmas decoration to bring good luck.

Ornamentation of a dwelling with greenery was believed to bring good fortune long before the Christian era. The Romans decorated their houses with laurel and bay at the Kalends of January (bay, of course, being sacred to Apollo and his son, Aesculapius, god of medicine) in protection against disease, while other pagan nations kept green boughs about them during the Winter Solstice. The sudden withering of bay, it may be added, was considered a death omen in Western thought: in *Richard II* (Act II, Sc iv) we have Shakespeare's Welsh captain saying:

> 'Tis thought the king is dead; we will not stay,
> The bay trees in our country are all wither'd.

In Wales, a cap made of hazel leaves and twigs was worn on the head for good luck, and was particularly efficacious if worn by sailors, or anyone connected with the sea and shipbuilding. Hazel, of course, was regarded as being a holy tree from pagan times when it was associated with fire and fertility, poetry and wisdom. Often, too, a hazel wand is used by water diviners and seekers of hidden veins of metal.

Wherever junipers grow man has sought supernatural protection, for according to Italian legend such a tree saved the infant Jesus during His flight from Herod into Egypt. Trees around Tal El-Basta and Belbeis, in Egypt, are still pointed out as those under which Jesus sheltered. According to 1 Kings, xix, 4–7, we learn that the juniper canopied Elijah in his flight from Queen Jezebel. Smoke from burning juniper logs has been used, too, in Europe to effect a cure for plague, fits, dropsy, liver trouble and, of course, to keep away the ubiquitous demons.

For a long time superstition has looked askance at lilac, specifically abhorring the white variety for household decoration. Even today, people avoid buying flower sprays containing lilac for friends in hospital, lest it cause a relapse or even death. It is considered very lucky, however, to find a five-petalled lilac blossom of any colour.

To the British, myrtle is the luckiest of trees, and was widely used to assure a girl's fecundity before the advent of orange blossoms. Should a garden have a vigorous blossoming of myrtle then a wedding was prophesied, while, in Wales, such a growth was held to show that harmony prevailed in the household.

Because the leaves of the poplar and the aspen tremble in the lightest current of air, they have been called *Shiver-trees*. Both were used in the cure of fevers and agues, particularly in Lincolnshire, where those who suffered from ague were told to nail a piece of their hair on an aspen and recite:

> Aspen-tree, aspen-tree
> I prithee shake and shiver for me.

While a fever might be cured by a piece of poplar bark in the hair:

> When Christ Our Lord was on the Cross,
> Then didst thou sadly shiver and toss.
> My aches and pains thou now must take,
> Instead of me I bid thee shake.

These two trees were condemned to shiver, the pious declared, because the aspen would not bow when Jesus passed, and the poplar shuddered when its thick branches went to make the Cross of Calvary.

Scottish folk-lore is rich with reference to the mountain-ash or rowan, 'Rowan-tree and red thread gar witches tyne their speed,' is one old Scottish saying. Some superstitious folk would not dream of entering a house which did not have the traditional chimney cross-beam of rowan, and some farmers would not touch a plough unless it had rowan handles. To scare away evil spirits, rowan crosses were tied to the tails of cattle in the Isle of Man, and in Yorkshire they used to say: 'If your whipstock's made of rowan, you may ride your nag through any town.'

By waving a wand of hawthorn and chanting this rhyme, the life of a Scottish cattle-thief was thought to be made easier:

> Cow's milk, and mare's milk,
> From every beast that bears milk.
> Harken to this voice o'mine,
> See thee now my hawthorn fine.
> Between St Johnston and Dundee,
> Come a' ye beasts, come a' to me.

Some other tree growths associated with Christians are holly, ivy, mistletoe and yew, although the latter was not used for house decoration because of its association with the dead.

Called the 'Golden Bough' in classical legend, mistletoe was sacred both to Christians and pagans, particularly the Celtic Druids, who cut their supplies for the winter and summer solstice festivals. To the Norsemen, mistletoe was deadly for it had slain their hero Baldur the Beautiful (an arrow of mistletoe flung by Loki), but it remained the plant of peace in ancient Scandinavian legend.

A thunder plant, mistletoe protected a house from the wrath of the gods and was chopped and boiled by housewife and witch alike as an antidote for poisons, and as a cure for epilepsy, St Vitus' Dance and various other ills. But many priests refused to have mistletoe in their churches even at Christmas time because of its pagan associations.

Kissing under the mistletoe is entirely an English custom and a convenient excuse for familiarity at office parties, but old-time superstitions about girls being barren if they had not been kissed under the mistletoe seem to have become lost in this age of plastic flowers.

For those who cut down mistletoe-bearing trees, death or misfortune were foretold and the Scottish family of Hay of

Errol, in Perthshire, had good reason to believe this. The prosperity of this family was assured, the old chronicles stated, so long as the old mistletoe-bearing oak near the Falcon Stone flourished. The Hays lost their land, the local folk averred, because they allowed the tree to perish; all around truly believing the verses traditionally attributed to Thomas Learmonth of Ercildoun (now Earlston) in Lauderdale, Scotland, called the Rhymer:

> . . . when the root of the aik (oak) decays,
> And the mistletoe dwines on its withered breast,
> The grass shall grow on Errol's hearthstone
> And the corbie roup in the falcon's nest.

Holly has always been considered a symbol of enduring life, and Christmas decorations would not seem complete without it. A strong protection against evil and thunder, holly was used as a remedy for chilblains, which were thrashed with a holly branch, 'to let the chilled blood out'.

Considered a kindly plant, ivy had ancient associations with the Roman god Bacchus, thus a sprig was often hung outside a vintner's or innkeeper's premises. Growing on a house, ivy would protect against witchcraft, or misfortune, and in Wales, in particular, should ivy wither on a house wall, financial loss was expected for the inmates.

Ivy was also used by lovers for divination in Herefordshire, Oxfordshire and in the south of Scotland, where this rhyme originates:

> Ivy, ivy, I love you
> In my bosom I put you,
> The first young man who speaks to me
> My future husband he shall be.

Various concoctions and essences of ivy were used in folk-medicine; for instance, juice of the ivy pushed inside the nostrils was a supposed cure for the common cold, while in Dorset such a lotion was used to cure skin diseases.

Connected with lightning, fire and clouds, the ash tree was considered by early man to be his original ancestor, and the mythologies of Scandinavia, and Greece expounded this idea. According to Norse mythology, the first man on earth was Askr, created from an ash tree by the gods; a wife being created for him from an aspen. This is one of the main reasons why witches chose ash as a wood for the dolls into which they stuck pins to cause a person's death.

All manner of cures have been attributed to the ash tree, from ruptures to pimples, but in Lincolnshire the ash tree which bore berries (called Sheder) was used to defeat the spells of warlocks, and the berry-less ones (Heder) for witches.

The winged seeds of the ash were said to forecast the death of a monarch by their failure to appear, while the leaves were used as love charms:

> Even-ash, even-ash, I pluck thee,
> This night my own true love to see,
> Neither in his rick nor in his rare,
> But in the clothes he does every day wear.

Birch garlands by the front door of a house kept away demons, while elder boughs attracted them. The elder has been linked with witchcraft for many centuries, and one curious superstition from Northamptonshire relates how a local witch may be uncovered. If a branch is cut from an elder tree, should the sap flow freely from the cut, look for a person with his or her arm bandaged to cover a new wound, for this person will be the witch sought after.

A stem of bracken was often used as a charm against witches because of the curious markings at its foot. These the pious identified with the CHI which is the first letter of the Greek form of Christ's name.

The traditional emblem of grief, the willow, is the symbol of those forsaken in love, and many jilted persons used to wear a willow wand as a note in John Aubrey's *Remaines of Gentilisme and*

53

Judaisme recounts: 'The young man whose late sweetheart is married to some other person does often in a frolique literally wear a willow garland, as I have seen in some parts of Oxfordshire.' The superstition was that the 'heart' of the willow would bear the grief.

Deeply venerated by the Norsemen and Celts, Druids and Indo-Europeans, the oak was considered blest with powers of peace and protection. According to Bede in his *Historia Ecclesiastica*, when St Augustine first preached before King Ethelbert of Kent on the Isle of Thanet, Ethelbert insisted that the sermon be delivered outside 'lest if they were skilful in sorcery, they might the rather deceive and prevail against him'. Ethelbert ensconsed himself under a massive oak tree just in case!

In pagan times, marriages were often celebrated under oaks and a special Marriage Oak was retained at Brampton, Cumberland, until the 1860s; for a bride and groom to embrace and dance under such a tree was considered lucky.

Of all the flora and herbs that are linked with superstition, henbane is perhaps the one most employed for evil spells. An extremely poisonous plant, which can cause temporary insanity and convulsions, it was supposed to assist clairvoyance and its leaves were burnt to invoke the spirits of darkness. From Welsh superstition we have the idea that if a child fell asleep near the plant, he would never awaken again.

Hemlock, too, was associated with devil worship and a compound of it was thought to be used by witches for transvection. In the English counties of Durham, Cumberland, Northumberland and Westmorland, it was known as the 'Devil's Oats', a mouthful of which made a man Satan's servant for life. Hemlock was also used in poultices against rheumatism.

The ghostly form of her future husband was the sight promised to the girl who mowed hempseed with a scythe in a churchyard. Timorously, the girls of Oxfordshire and the Welsh Border scaled the churchyard wall on All Hallow's Eve; borrowed the sexton's scythe, and took turns at cutting the hempseed and peering into the dark shadows of the vaults for a glimpse of their future spouses. As they cut they incanted this spell:

> Hempseed I sow, Hempseed I mow,
> He that's to marry me,
> Come after me and mow.

Ferns known as 'Adder's Tongue' (or 'Adder's Spear'), because of the yellow-green spikes were formerly gathered when the moon was waning. The leaves of the plant could be made into a plaster to help cure swellings and tumours, but if drunk as an infusion conferred the gift of tongues.

Most ferns, however, were associated with thunder and lightning. In England, they were known as 'Devil's Brushes', while in Ireland their lack of blooms was attributed to a curse laid on them by St Patrick. Hung about houses they were thought to be a protection against tempests, but if burnt the superstition said it would bring on rain. In 1636, Lord Pembroke, Chamberlain to Charles I, commanded the High Sheriff of Staffordshire, in the King's name, that to ensure fine weather no fern should be burnt during the sovereign's visit.

A plant of great mystery and magical repute is the mandrake, known since remote times for image mysticism. No man ever pulled its bifurcated roots himself if he could possibly help it, and one way of collecting it was to tie a hungry dog to the plant after the soil round the roots had been loosened with an ivory or iron tool. With a piece of food placed just outside its reach, the dog would strain and eventually pull the mandrake out of the earth. Meanwhile the gatherer had retired out of earshot, for the mandrake was thought to utter a death-curse as it left the earth. After a while the gatherer would return to untie the mandrake from the dog's harness, and many are the stories of dogs who were found dead beside the uprooted mandrake. The plant was also sought after by barren women for fertility, as we read in Genesis, xxx, 14–17, in the story of Rachel.

Milfoil (or yarrow) tied to a cradle protected a baby as well as its mother. In Kent, particularly, the plant was used as a love charm:

Yarrow, sweet yarrow, the first that I have found
In the name of Jesus, I pluck thee from the ground.
As Jesus loved sweet Mary, and took her for his dear,
So in a dream tonight I pray, my lover to appear.

Beans have had a curious history of superstition and are usually associated with ghosts and funerals. The Romans both ate and scattered beans at funerals and at North Country interments broad beans were buried with the coffin, so that the souls of the departed could live on in the flowers.

Miners of the English Midlands have been known to attribute pit accidents to the baleful influence of broad beans, while in Leicestershire they were supposed to give nightmares—which they probably did! According to a Buckinghamshire superstition, should one white bean grow in a row then the grower's family were due for a bereavement.

Said to be imbued with the power of making a person invisible, chicory was hung on the banners of those making a crusade or exploring a new land; many a prospector on his way to California in search for gold had a carrot-like chicory root in his pocket for luck. With the moonwart and springwort, chicory was thought to be useful for opening locks or removing obstacles, especially if it had been gathered at midnight on 25 July (St James's Day).

Beronice, the woman healed by Christ of haemorrhage, is said to have given her name to Betony, a plant the superstitious alleged was in constant enmity with the vine, as the tendrils of the latter always curled in the opposite direction. According to the *Anglo-Saxon Leech Book*: 'Betony is good whether for the man's soul or his body, and to shield him against monstrous nocturnal visitors, and frightful visions and dreams (ie, caused by booze!).'

At one time almost every girl carried a list of good- and bad-luck flowers in her purse, and from a selection of ladies' mystic books of the seventeenth century come these words of superstitious wisdom:

BRIONY: 'If to childe-bede thou wouldst goe, dust thy food with brionie.'

CELANDINE: Useful for healing jaundice, poor sight and warts.

COWSLIPS: Good for loss of memory and love charms.
> 'Tisty, tosty tell me true
> Who is he that I shall woo.'

CYCLAMEN: A serviceable emetic and an aid to a girl recovering from the shock of being jilted.

DOCK: The common antidote to the nettle:
> 'Out nettle in dock,
> Dock shall have a new frock,
> But nettle shall have none.'

FOXGLOVE: A fairy plant, to be avoided, called in many parts 'Dead man's fingers'.

LADY'S SMOCK: Also known as 'cuckoo flower,' must never be put in a bouquet or garland.

LILY: Although a symbol of virginity, the lily was also an omen of death. Planted in a garden they kept ghosts away.

MARIGOLD: A good protection for a girl against witchcraft; especially if taken at breakfast as a conserve.

MEADOWSWEET: Very unlucky because it was thought to promote a 'deathe-sleepe'.

MUGWORT: A wonderful charm for travellers.

NIGHTSHADE (*Atropa Belladonna*): A deadly poison. Used by witches in their flying-ointments, thought to make a house a ruin within ten years.

ORPINE: Ensured a long life if gathered at Midsummer's Eve.

PASQUE FLOWER: A purple anemone thought to grow where blood had been spilt.

PEONY: Good for wounds in the heart, and used in Ireland to counter the after-pains of childbirth.

PERIWINKLE: Associated with death and witchcraft; the usual mock crown for criminals in the Middle Ages on their way to the gallows.

POPPY: Makes a girl fertile. Also drives away unwanted lovers.

PRIMROSE: Unlucky to bring a handful into the house. Drives away witches.

ROSE: The symbol of love. If a girl placed a rose on Midsummer's Eve under her pillow, she would haunt her lover's dreams.

SNOWDROP: Emblem of hope, but considered unlucky as a house decoration.

VIOLET: Usually considered unlucky; but to dream of violets meant a change for the better in circumstances.

Superstitions have not been forgotten either in the fruit or vegetable garden.

Oranges, commonly called 'love fruit', have figured in the making of love potions and fertility concoctions since the dawn of civilisation. In Britain, the orange's magic powers seem to date from the fruit gardens of the Stuarts, when orange blossoms began to supersede myrtle and rosemary for wedding decorations. At one time, in Norfolk, the present of an orange between lovers was believed to ensure requited love.

According to another tradition, it is considered unlucky to eat (or gather) blackberries after 11 October (Old Michaelmas Day), for it was on this day, the wise recounted, that Satan fell into a blackberry thicket and cursed the bush which had scratched him so painfully. Mirroring a similar belief in Normandy, the people of Ross-on-Wye, in Herefordshire, for long never ate blackberries at all for fear of being poisoned by the saliva the Devil was said to have spattered upon them.

Brambles, however, were much sought after for their curative powers and up to late in the last century were used for sick cattle (especially if the beasts were inflicted with muscular pain, thought to be brought on by the evil influences of the shrew mouse). Rheumatism, boils, rickets, blackheads, whooping-cough and eczema were all thought to be curable by crawling through a bramble bush (the same was said of maple branches for children's diseases). In Cornwall, burns were treated with bramble-leaves, while this verse was recited:

> There came three angels out of the East,
> One brought Fire and two brought Frost.
> In the name of the Father, Son and Holy Ghost.

Apples were frequently used as charms and omens:

> A bloom on the tree when the apples are ripe
> Is a sure termination of somebody's life.

ran the saying which is probably as old as the pagan idea that Heaven would be like a Vale of Apple Trees. Poultices used to be made of rotten apples for the cure of rheumatism, and a sure cure for warts, so the house almanacs related, was to cut an apple in two, rub the wart with both halves, tie them together and bury the whole in the ground, the wart disappearing as the apple rotted. Apple spells were common in Warwickshire and Shropshire:

> If a fine spell thou wishes to weave,
> Take an apple from a man's neive (hand).
> Eat a good bite and return it to him
> Revenge will be thine ere the Sun dim.

In Cornwall, at Hallowmass, neighbours and families gave each other presents of large apples. Named 'Allan Apples' these were deemed to bring good luck. Should a young unmarried girl sleep with one under her pillow she would dream of her future husband.

Apple-wassailing was a Christmas custom in many parts of the West Country of England, or on New Year's Eve in Sussex. Usually, men, women and children went to the orchard they wished to propitiate and banged drums, blew trumpets and made an almighty din to drive the demons away from the topmost branches of the apple trees. When this had been done, an apple-gathering ceremony was mimed in the hope that, come harvest time, the good spirits of the trees would remember the acts of kindness (donations of cider and cake to the tree) and produce an abundance of fruit. Sometimes the trees were serenaded:

> Hail to thee, old Apple Tree,
> Stand fast root, bear well top,
> Pray God send us a good howling crop.
> Every twig, apples big,
> Every bow, apples enow,
> Hats full, caps full,
> and pockets full too.

Another old superstition held that only one day in the year was good for planting potatoes, and that was Good Friday. For upon that day alone the Devil had no power for evil over the soil. But not every person held this view, and many then as now were greatly averse to breaking ground on the anniversary of the Crucifixion.

Potatoes were also carried around until they were rotten as a cure for rheumatism, while carrots not only cured rheumatism, asthma, gallstones and croup, but were an essential ingredient of love potions and philtres to strengthen the eyesight. While peas were used in Cornwall for curing warts, in Derbyshire their straw was rubbed on the clothes of a girl who had not been kissed on St Valentine's Day so that her future love-life would not be entirely blighted. Young men on the Scottish

Borders counted peas in a pod, much the same as girls still do today with prune stones, for 'tinker, tailor, soldier, sailor,' and so on.

Lettuce, both wild and cultivated, was considered dangerous to women as it was thought to induce barrenness, and in Richmond, Surrey, a woman carefully counted the number of lettuces in her garden for fear that too many would make her sterile. The Romans, however, kept lettuce by as a titbit at banquets and considered them efficacious in countering drunkenness and in promoting potency in sexual games after the feast. Our Anglo-Saxon ancestors used lettuce (Sleep-wort) as a cure for insomnia, while the mighty god-king Rameses II is still to be seen on his tomb murals offering lettuce to the pantheon of ancient Egyptian gods.

Onions have been employed for centuries as anti-witch and anti-snake amulets, or for lovers' divinations. Again, scholars believed that an onion rubbed on the hand deadened the pain of a cane's swipe, an extension of the primitive belief that onions ('witches' apples') would drive away evil of all kinds.

In ancient Greece, parsley was associated with death, and graves were strewn with the bright-green herb, but if sown on Good Friday, the later Christians averred, it was a very lucky plant. Perhaps the strangest of all superstitions about parsley was the idea that to transplant its roots would bring speedy death to someone in the close vicinity; for this reason no one would transplant parsley in Gloucester.

Superstitions about sage, however, were concerned with its ability to impart wisdom, and the plant was used to strengthen the memory. Any garden in which sage grew profusely was regarded by country folk to belong to a woman who was strong of will—one man in Oxford cut down a vigorous growth of sage in his garden because he said he didn't want people to think that his wife was the 'boss'.

The souls of the departed were once thought to have dwelt in the leaves of thyme, so that the herb was often associated with the ghosts of murdered people. In folk-medicine, it was believed to give courage and tenacity. Most other superstitions connected with thyme have something or other to do with death, and sprigs of the plant were often dropped on a coffin before it was lowered into the grave.

Weeds were thought by many to be God's curse on the land for Adam's first disobedience. As late as 1900, people in Suffolk quickened their pace when passing a garden full of weeds.

6

Mystery in Symbols

Social life is impossible without communication and just as a simple word can, with the passage of time, gather round it many associations and a variety of meanings, so can a symbol.

The human mind unconsciously compares everything the eyes see with what has already been stored in the memory centres of the brain. Among the most important symbols of all are those of belief and superstition, and a glimpse of a certain symbol was enough to gladden or terrorise the hearts of our ancestors.

Astarte, the Mesopotamian goddess of love, for instance, was usually depicted wearing a crescent moon head-dress, which, because of the resemblance to horns, had sexual overtones.

A few more examples will make the pattern clear:

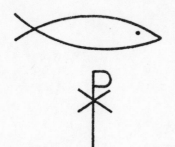

These are two Christian signs, the sign of the fish and the *Chi-Roh*, the first two letters of the Greek word for Christ.

Symbols, too, were used in the conveyance of a spiritual-occult message:

Tau cross with Greek letters from the beginning and the end of the alphabet meant—*I am the Alpha and Omega of life*—the beginning and the end.

'Ι	ησους	The initial letters of the Greek	JESUS
Χ	ριστος	description of Christ is spelt	CHRIST
Θ	εόυ	out in the word for fish	OF GOD
Υ	ιος		SON
Σ	ωτηρ		SAVIOUR

Symbolic images, too, form one of the most ancient facets of magic. In early instances wax or clay figures, the forerunners of present-day photographs or portraits in the case of human images, were frequently used for evil purposes; although images have also been used for a variety of other purposes, from increasing wealth, to making a barren woman fertile.

The usual method was to make a figure (in wax, metal or clay) roughly resembling the person to be assisted or damned. To make the spell more potent, something that belonged to the person was added, such as a piece of hair, the thread from a coat, a paring of a finger-nail and so on.

When the image was made, the incantation for good or evil was recited. Sometimes a spell or incantation was written down on a piece of parchment for extra potency with a border of accompanying symbols. Such a spell might read:

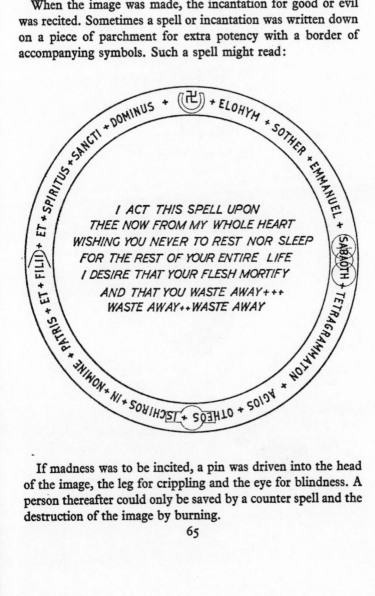

If madness was to be incited, a pin was driven into the head of the image, the leg for crippling and the eye for blindness. A person thereafter could only be saved by a counter spell and the destruction of the image by burning.

Of the world's most common occult symbols the following are but a few. Modern witchcraft uses an amalgam of many symbols relating to different cultures.

Buddhist and Eastern Symbols

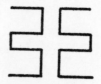

Buddhist Double Axe
Divine Power

OM-MAN-NI PAD-ME-HUM
Tibetan Mantra of Chennasee

| *Snake and Bamboo* | *Siva* | *Vishnu* | *Brahma* |
| Wisdom | Destruction | The Preserver | Creation |

The Gourd of Taoist
Necromancy

Ying Yang—Creation
Principle

Trimurti

Ancient magical symbols are the basis for the flag of South Korea; the circle and groups of lines dividing according to the traditional rules of magic.

Christian Symbols

Crosses have been used by man as symbols since very early times; they do not appear only as Christian emblems. Here are those most commonly used for magical purposes.

The Heart, Flame, Cross, Passion Flower, Ship and Candle are all used as Christian symbols, usually with the inscription: IESUS HOMINUM SALVATOR (Christ, the saviour of man), or, I(ESUS) N(AZARENUS) R(EX) I(UDAEORUM) (Jesus of Nazareth King of Jews).

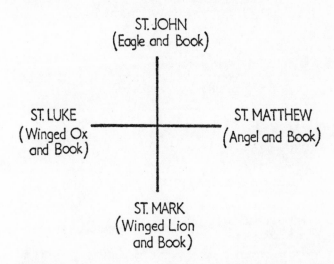

ST. JOHN
(Eagle and Book)

ST. LUKE
(Winged Ox and Book)

ST. MATTHEW
(Angel and Book)

ST. MARK
(Winged Lion and Book)

The Bible, and Bible and Key have been used a great deal in Christian divination, particularly for the detection of thieves.

Should a girl from St Cloud, Minnesota, wish to find out if she was to marry, she took the front door key of her house and inserted it in the Bible at the *Song of Solomon*. The Bible was then tightly bound with her stocking. The girl then supported the Bible by placing her two third fingers under the key. If, while she recited a chosen text from the *Song of Solomon*, the

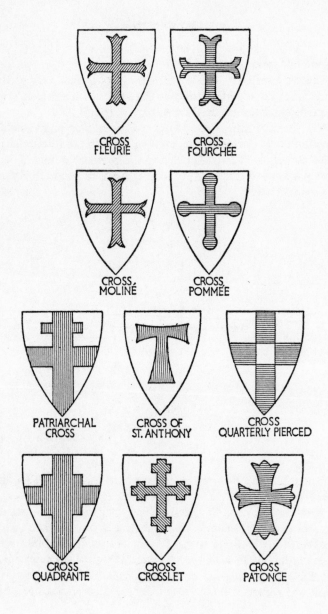

CROSS
FLEURIE

CROSS
FOURCHÉE

CROSS,
MOLINE

CROSS,
POMMÉE

PATRIARCHAL
CROSS

CROSS OF
ST. ANTHONY

CROSS
QUARTERLY PIERCED

CROSS
QUADRANTE

CROSS
CROSSLET

CROSS
PATONCE

Bible turned under her supporting fingers she would marry soon; if nothing happened she would die a spinster.

People have used the Bible also to forecast 'luck' for the whole year. Should the superstitious enquirer from Richmond, in Yorkshire, or Richmond, in Virginia, where this was once widely believed, take the Bible on New Year's morning, let it fall on a table and stab the page falling open with the finger at random, the verse thus blindly chosen was said to foretell the year's fortune. This practice was adopted whenever guidance was sought.

The story goes that King Charles I of England was persuaded to have his fortune told thus. Charles, fundamentally a superstitious man, assented and to his horror turned up a verse prophesying his own death and the loss of his kingdom. Trying to laugh it off as a joke, his companion, Lord Falkland, also tried his luck; he, too, turned up a death omen. Lord Falkland was killed at the Battle of Newbury in 1643, and Charles was executed six years later.

Divination

Aeromancy: Weathercock symbol; used by the superstitious to divine the future by studying wind and weather.

Gastromancy: Crystal Ball.

Astrology: Witches' Hats.

Hydromancy: Goblet sign surrounded by seven lit candles. Divination by means of liquids.

Augury: Symbol of eagle with serpent in mouth. Divination by observation of birds and serpents.

Necromancy: Two candles in sticks on draped table with accompanying skull and cross-bones.

Capnomancy: Skull surrounded by smoke in a vase for divination by smoke.

Pyromancy: Symbol of a brazier for fortune-telling by fire.

Chiromancy: Human hand symbol with palmistry lines drawn out.

The Symbolism of Ancient Egypt

The Eye: In common with the superstitions of most following ages, the ancient Egyptians looked upon the eye as a strong vehicle of spiritual power; a potency by which the evil intended could be made to possess another merely by a glance. From this we have the term 'overlooked', which was often applied to those who were thought to have fallen under some enchantment.

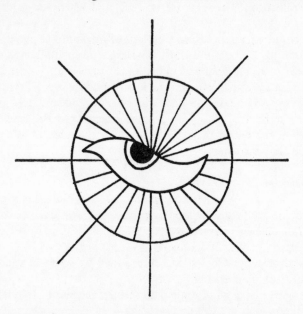

This was a superstition as common in Phillipsburg, Kansas, as it was in Middlesbrough, in England, or in Thebes, in Egypt. Charms against these 'overlookings' were innumerable (a cross, a wheel, a crescent moon, or a serpent); in Egypt a blue beard was worn for protection. As worshippers of the Sun, the ancient Egyptians often inscribed their monuments with sun discs in conjunction with the eye. Because of its ancient divinity, it was unlucky to point at the sun, but those born at sunrise were deemed very lucky indeed, being under the personal protection of the first Egyptian god to achieve nation-wide recognition, Re.

The *Tet* of Osiris, 'highest of all powers', and divine King of Egypt symbolised stability. All hope of immortality among the Egyptians was bound up in Osiris. A *Dad* amulet with this symbol was often placed on the neck of a mummy for protection.

The Egyptian concept of the sky was that of a vast ocean, and they represented the sun disc as sailing across this ocean in a

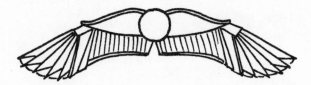

bark. A *Horbehutel* symbol was usually placed over gates and doors of temples as a protection against destruction.

Traditionally the enemy of the sun-god of Egypt, the *winged serpent* figures in a great number of tomb murals. Not always a sign of evil, three types of serpent appear; uraeus (*cobra di capello*)—a symbol of divine-royal sovereignty, the asp, or cerastes, and the coluber.

71

Many royal personages had the symbolism *Nefer* for good luck in their names: Nefertari (Aahames-Nefertari) sister-wife of the eighteenth-dynasty pharaoh, Aahames I, Nefer-ka-Rā, ninth king of the third dynasty, and the fabulously beautiful Nefertiti, wife of Akhnaton.

Akh or *Khu*, the symbolic rising sun of Osiris. A birth amulet representing the sun's disc rising from the horizon.

Ab—the soul symbol; sign of the *Ba* or *Ka*.

The *Scarab* (Beetle) of longevity.

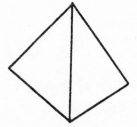

Pyramid, symbol of heavenly fire.

Sistrum of Isis. The sistrum, a musical instrument formed of a loop of bronze ribbon fastened to handle, crossed by three or four metal bands passing through holes in each side of the loop, was one of the usual attributes of goddesses (particularly Hathor, the horned-cow goddess of heavenly love and joy). A great enchantress, Isis, wife of Osiris, sometimes merged with Hathor.

Falcon—spirit of the sun. Symbols of Horus, the falcon-headed god, usually show him with an *ankh* (see p. 74) in his right hand. Son of Isis and Osiris, Horus was personally identified with the king; each succeeding pharaoh used the name Horus as the first of his titles.

73

Menat (Home, Virility, Family), a sign of divine protection, the sight of which was supposed to drive away care. Most used in Saite times, fifth name of Lower Egypt.

Ankh (Life), one of the most important of all Ancient Egyptian superstitious symbols, although difficult to interpret, whether 'life' here, or 'life' after death. It is sometimes found in combination with the *dad*.

Utchat (Health), usually inscribed on an amulet for wrist or arm, mostly against spoken curses or malice. Again (if in pairs) used to represent the Eyes of Horus, in some instances one for L (moon) and one for R (sun).

Heha—or *Neh*—Divine Protection, used as a pectoral.

74

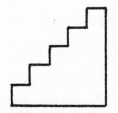

Stairs. Probably signified the way to the throne of Osiris; the way up to heaven.

Buckle of Isis (Protection). This symbol was usually made up of some red material, such as jasper, porphyry, or carnelian (ie, for the blood of Isis, which washes away the sins of the wearer); usually a red ornament for the dead.

Sma—the mystic symbol of union.

Frog, the superstitious symbol of abundance; used after the XVIIIth dynasty.

75

Mut. Usually a symbol made of gold. It represented to the superstitious the protection of Isis.

Usekh. Collar symbol of gold. Given to a mummy for power to remove bandages.

Urs. The headrest. Usually made of hematite, this object symbolised support.

Shen, the mystic symbol of enduring life.

Uaz. Lotus, creation, or eternal youth.

User, royal sceptre, signifying to the credulous, Heaven and Earth.

76

The Plummet, the mystic symbol inscribed to assure justice, moderation and wisdom under the law.

Gnosticism

This was a spiritual and metaphysical system, antecedent to Christianity, which sought to combine Oriental religions with Greek philosophy. In time, orthodox Christianity developed gnostic heresies and Gnosticism assumed Christian forms. By AD 600 Gnosticism had lost its hold, but the superstitious still used gnostic symbols of which the following were the most prominent: 'the Mystic Star' (a heptagram), 'Creation' (an octagram), 'Sigil of the Sun', 'Water-Fire principle', 'Abraxas' (much worn during the Middle Ages as an amulet), 'Sigil of the World' and the 'Seven-Headed Serpent'.

Good Luck

Here are the 'top fifteen' good luck symbols:

Billieken	Cricket	Shoe
Dog	Crescent	Three Monkeys
Carp	Crossed Fingers	Wheel
Sweep	Clover	Wishing Well
Dice	Quartrefoil	Toadstool

Nordic

Modern witches still use Nordic signs and symbols in their practices, with these five as the most employed: acorn (longevity), anvil (creation), horns (a moon sign of power, usually in the form of a Viking helmet), Thor's hammer, wheel and cross (eternity). Also the magic Nordic letters:

77

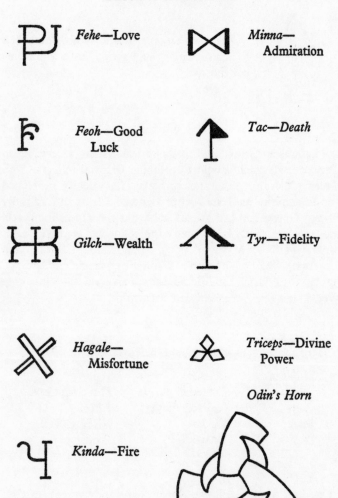

Fehe—Love

Minna—
    Admiration

Feoh—Good
    Luck

Tac—Death

Gilch—Wealth

Tyr—Fidelity

Hagale—
    Misfortune

Triceps—Divine
    Power

Odin's Horn

Kinda—Fire

78

Japanese Symbols

In the same way that some Westerners avoid spilling salt and the number thirteen, the Japanese evade thirty-three (*san-zan*, 'unescapable misfortunes') and the possibility of dropping rice carelessly, the latter act being liable, it is believed, to risk a famine. As a nation, the Japanese are also much taken with soothsaying, and fortune-tellers, *eki-sha*, can be found everywhere.

A symbol of great power which soon manifests itself to Westerners is the *torii*. *Torii* (cf Indian, *torana*, Chinese, *p'ai-lou*, Korean, *hong-sal-mun*), the gateway of purification, is seen at the entrance to all Shinto shrines, of which there are more than 100,000 in Japan.

A popular superstition is that the *torii* is the first stage in purification, for 'the god-gate expels the darkness from the heart'. The origin of the *torii* is unknown, but scholars have suggested that the word is derived from the Sanskrit *torana*, which means 'bird perch'. Fanciful tales do tell of how in ancient times the *torii* were the perches for sacred birds (the long-necked flying cocks).

Animals of the Zodiac, which play an important role in Japanese life were until quite recently used to indicate the time of day or night. They are:

Rat	Nezumi	N	12 Noon, or Midnight
Ox	Ushi	NNE	1 o'clock
Tiger	Tora	ENE	2 o'clock
Hare	Usagi	E	and so on
Dragon	Tatsu	ESE	
Snake	Hebi	SSE	
Horse	Uma	S	
Sheep	Hitsuji	SSW	
Monkey	Saru	WSW	
Cock	Tori	W	
Dog	Inu	WNW	
Boar	Inoshishi	NNW	

79

Each animal had its own special superstition; the dog, for instance, was thought to help women during pregnancy, while the boar was thought to give courage and audacity. Sometimes a person might carry a good-luck amulet about with him bearing the animal sign for the hour of his birth: ie, the tiger, if he had been born at two o'clock in the morning.

Some Talisman Inscriptions

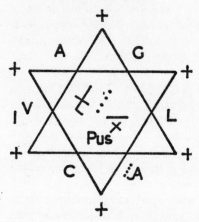

For making a wizard's clothes auspicious

A Crusader's talisman

A triangle which protects
against blindness

Another against illness
generally

A		M
B		N
C		O
D		R
E		S
F, P, Ph		T, Ts, Th
G		
H		
I, J, Y		U, V
K, Q		X
L		Z

The Magic Alphabet
82

7

Beware the Living and the Dead

As one of the most indestructible parts of the body, human hair has attracted around it a miscellany of superstitions. Free and luxuriant hair growths have always been associated with strength but were thought by some to indicate that the owners were likely to be lacking in wit. A life of great riches was prophesied for the man with hairy arms, but the sudden loss of hair through illness was supposed to foretell the sudden death of one of the afflicted's family.

In some districts lank hair was held to denote a cunning nature, and curly hair to show inner serenity and a cheerful temperament. Dark hair was considered lucky, especially for 'First Footers', but there has always been a curious prejudice against red hair. This has been attributed to the belief that Judas Iscariot, Christ's betrayer, had red hair, but may equally derive from lingering folk-memory of the rapacious red-haired Danish pirates who once haunted England's coasts. Red hair is also commonly supposed to be a sign of ungovernable temper, while people in Dumbartonshire, in Scotland, still say that a man with red hair will prove an unfaithful husband.

At Portland, Maine, in USA, they used to declare:

> Beware of that man,
> Be he friend or brother,
> Whose hair is one colour
> And moustache another.

Hair cutting, too, had its old superstitions:

> Best never been born if Sunday shorn,
> And likewise leave out Monday.
> Cut Thursday or Saturday you'll never grow rich,
> But live long if cut on a Tuesday.
> Shear a beast on Wednesday morn,
> And mankind on a Friday.

It was important, too, for hair clippings to be burnt, for any evilly disposed person (particularly in the Far East) could work black magic against the owner, with just a small clipping. Should hair clippings burn bright a long life was assured, but if they smouldered misfortune was to be expected. Illness, too, could be cured if a hair from the head of the afflicted was thrown into the wind, the hair carrying the ill with it.

Teeth are another source of superstition and it was believed to be a bad omen if a baby was born with teeth, whether a few or just one. Some held it meant that the child would meet a violent death, others that it would grow up to become a murderer. Teething troubles also had their omens and various teething rings of magical power were donated by friends. Mostly of coral, in the form of necklaces or bangles, these were sometimes braided with donkey hair for extra potency.

In past ages extracted teeth were generally retained until the death of the owner, and often buried with him in his coffin.

If not, the teeth were burned to keep witches from using their shells for the lodgement of evil.

A tooth taken from a dead man's skull was particularly sought after as a charm against toothache. If suspended in a bag over a fireplace with a mole's foot and this written charm, it was thought to give protection to the whole family:

Peter sat upon a marble stone,
When Jesus passed him by.
'Oh Lord,' quoth Peter, 'my tooth doth ache.'
'Peter thou art whole,' said the Lord.
Those who keep these words by them
Shall never have toothache.

Long fingers are supposed to belong to a spendthrift, or a thief, and if the forefinger was as long as the second finger, or longer, it was a sure sign of dishonesty. The forefinger of the right hand was once called the Poison Finger, while the third finger of the left hand was considered to have healing powers. A child born with more than five fingers was lucky indeed, and probably a prodigy of some sort.

In 1812 an eight-year-old American boy, Zerah Colburn, was brought to London to show his great mathematical skill. The Duke of Gloucester quizzed him and was amazed when, after a pause of a second or two, the boy gave him the correct answer for 21,734 multiplied by 543, namely 11,801,562; the boy was reputed to have five fingers on each hand!

Finger-nails, according to superstition, should be pared only on certain days (Monday and Tuesday) as with hair, and for extra protection against the powers of evil it should be done over an open Bible. Marks on the nails, too, were often given an occult significance, a spot appearing on the fourth finger being held to foretell a journey, or a yellow spot death.

Tears of genuine grief were greatly feared among certain societies, especially at funerals. The superstitious said that tears kept the dead earthbound and unable to find peace, and in

Ireland it was recommended that tears should be held back until a person had been dead at least three hours, so enabling the soul to escape from the earthly plane. Tears were thought particularly unlucky at baptisms and weddings, but lucky if the baby or bride cried at these functions.

The human hand, man's first tool, has always been credited with spiritual as well as physical powers, as witness the old belief that kings and emperors, prelates and faith healers, had only to touch a person to work magic. Palmistry, of course, has fostered the idea that the hand is the mirror of a man's life and in earlier days the touch of a dead man's hand was claimed as a certain cure for skin blemishes and various tumours.

Urine, like hair, blood and excreta, was said to have potential magical properties and the superstitious often boiled urine to break spells they believed had been cast upon them. And some country folk still use urine to heal chilblains and chapped hands.

Idiots, once common in closely in-bred communities, were considered to be God's children, a belief charitably applied to most other afflicted people. At one time 'silly' meant 'blessed' and the babblings of the mentally deranged were taken for spirit voices. Dumb persons were credited with a foot in both worlds, but the cross-eyed were generally feared, especially by Spanish bullfighters!

Not so long ago, as soon as it was evident that a person's life was nearing its end, various superstitious rites were commonly performed. Essentially the idea was to ease the passing of life, which was considered a difficult process. Locks, bolts and staples were all released and doors and windows opened, knots were untied and mirrors reversed so that the reflection of the soul would not be for ever trapped in the glass. Should the bed in which the dying one rested lie crosswise to the floorboards (or beams of the ceiling), it was turned to be parallel.

Pillows of game birds' feathers, blankets of foreign (ie not made in the locality) manufacture were removed as death was held impossible while they remained. Emily Brontë used this superstition in *Wuthering Heights*, when she portrayed Catherine Earnshaw (Linton) saying, 'Ah! they put pigeon's feathers in the pillow—no wonder I couldn't die.' Today, some of the methods once used to ease death, like tying coloured tape round the dying person's neck, could well invite a charge of murder or homicide.

There used to be an ancient notion that, immediately after death, the corpse needed special protection until the soul reached the 'other side'. Green turf wrapped in paper and placed by the dead person's leg was one device to help an exit, and sometimes a bucket of salt water was placed under the bed or bier and a lighted candle placed on the corpse's chest. In the Scottish Lowlands, when the corpse had been laid out, the oldest relative approached the bier, took a lighted candle, waved it three times over the corpse, and then sprinkled it with salt. Sometimes food was left near the corpse for the soul's last repast.

In many parts it was the custom never to leave the dead alone in a room without people or candles (never animals), as everyone knew that the evil spirits attracted to corpses were afraid of light. Various superstitions surrounded these corpse lights; often the soul was considered to inhabit the candle flame for a while, and even when the candle had burnt out there were those who claimed that they could still see the flame burning.

This constant company of the dead was in much the same tradition as the 'wakes' or corpse-watching ceremonies which were all common in many parts of the country. In Scotland and Ireland, these wakes were often very boisterous affairs which people travelled many miles to attend. For hours they would dance and sing round the coffined body, eating large quantities of food and quaffing whisky as a mark of respect to the hospitality of the dead.

Death was expected at certain times more than others, for instance, at the waning of the moon and at ebb-tide. It may be remembered that in *David Copperfield*, by Charles Dickens, Peggoty remarks, 'People can't die along the coast except when the tide's pretty near out. They can't be born unless it's pretty nigh in.' In some parishes the state of the tide was recorded in death registers.

Formerly, it was believed that the living would have a firmer hold on this life if they touched the dead, and in many parts visitors who knew the deceased in life were invited (and expected) to touch the corpse. In Scotland, this ritual touching was thought to prevent haunting, and derived from an even older ritual employed to prove innocence. It was widely believed that the corpse of a murdered person would bleed (or rise up) at the touch of the murderer's hand, and all suspects therefore were subjected to the ordeal of touching the dead.

When arrangements were being made for the funeral, it was considered dangerous for the corpse to be left with the eyes open, for whoever came into the dead man's sight was doomed to follow him soon to the grave. Often coins were placed on a dead man's eyes to keep them shut, mirroring also the old idea that one must pay a toll to enter the next world.

In some districts it was thought necessary to tie the feet of a corpse together to stop a demon entering the body. It was also considered a wise precaution against the same risk to be buried in linen, but a woman could be buried in her wedding dress and the man in his best overcoat so long as any pins or buttons were removed; if not their ghosts might go a-haunting.

Household goods, too, were once buried with the dead in the belief that they would be needed in the after life, the custom of the Egyptians being the best-known example. Even in this twentieth-century world, various trinkets still find their way for superstitious reasons into coffins; toys for children, and jewellery, books and favourite articles for adults. In Sweden, mirrors were placed in the coffins of dead girls, so that they could tidy their hair on Judgment Day.

It was once thought unlucky to stand in the sun when attending a funeral in case one was marked out as the next to die; and meeting a funeral when out for a walk has always been considered an unfavourable omen. But in Ireland warts could be cured by wishing hard as a funeral passed. Another very persistent superstition is that death never makes less than three visitations to a community.

To be the first to be buried in a new cemetery was tantamount to landing straight in the Devil's lap and there are many records of the corpse of a dead vagrant, criminal, or even an animal, having been preserved in order to open up a new cemetery. Similarly the last person to be interred was thought to be doomed as the eternal guardian of that cemetery.

A curious blend of pagan and Christian superstition held that a corpse must be complete when buried to avoid embarrassing consequences in the next world. Thus people who had had a limb amputated often kept it pickled to be buried with them, so that God could eventually reunite them in full working order.

To carry a corpse out of a house in any position but feet first was thought to imperil the immortality of the deceased's soul, and it was also preferable that the funeral procession should travel in a sunwise direction. If a church or a market cross was encountered on the way, it was considered best to carry the coffin once round the area. There was also a widespread but quite unfounded belief that if a corpse was carried over private land a public right of way was established for ever. In some parts of the country certain roads and paths were designated Corpse Roads so that other public highways should not become affected by bad luck.

Graves were usually laid out running from east to west so that, facing the east, the deceased would be able to rise with the sun on the Day of Judgment; a north–south position was considered a severe handicap. Again, it was bad luck to tread on a grave, and if it happened to be that of an unbaptised or stillborn child the offender was more than likely to fall victim to the mystic disease of 'gravemerelles'.

Other churchyard acts of ill omen were to leave a churchyard gate open on a Sunday, to leave a newly-dug grave gaping, or to move gravestones and monuments. Some folk still say that a church will fall into disuse if ever the graveslabs from its churchyard are used as paving stones. As for disturbing the dead, there were many who said that disturbing the body of Scottish poet, Robert Burns, when he was re-interred in the Burns Mausoleum at St Michael's Churchyard, Dumfries, in 1815, would mean the premature death of all Burns' surviving relatives!

At Abbotts Ann, in Hampshire, maidens' garlands used to be carried at the funeral of an unmarried woman. After the ceremony, the garlands were left to hang inside the church until they dropped, and were then buried in the churchyard. To remove the garlands before they fell was to invite the worst of bad luck.

From earliest times, human bones have been thought to be a medium for psychic power, and down the centuries all kinds of bones have been used for healing purposes, for making charms and as aids to divination. In Britain, the blade-bone of a sheep was for long treasured for its allegedly magical properties, while in Africa the small bones of domestic animals are still regularly used by witch-doctors for detecting criminals and casting death spells.

In the Middle Ages, epileptics were often given ground skull-bone mixed in with their food as a cure, the theory being that since the skull was one of the places the soul was thought to inhabit, a cure was assured. And when, early in Elizabeth I's reign, a number of Easterlings (German immigrants) fell ill while melting metal at the Royal Mint, London, they were advised that a certain cure would be found in drinking from a human skull. An order was obtained 'to take of the Headds Uppon London Bridge (where the heads of criminals and the like were displayed as an example to others) and make cuppes thereof, whereof they dranke and founde some relief, althoughe the mooste of them dyed'.

  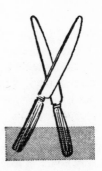

8

Animal Superstitions

Of all the world's snakes the one which seems to have attracted most superstitions to itself is the adder. Always a creature of ill omen, it was thought to be doubly dangerous if found dead, for then the life of he who first discovered it was said to be forfeit to the snake. However, to kill the first adder seen in spring was considered lucky, and particularly so if the fatal blow was dealt with an ash stick.

The skin of a dead adder was once thought to have medicinal value and was worn in the hat to prevent headaches, and round the limbs as protection against rheumatism. The fat of the adder was retained as an antidote for bites. Like other snakes, an adder, it is still believed, cannot die before the sun goes down.

Another popular belief among countrymen was that if a lizard saw a snake approach a sleeping man it would promptly wake the sleeper. Hence lizards were generally looked upon with favour, but not if they crossed the path of a bridal procession.

Toads are strong in superstition, and no self-respecting witch would be without one. Yet it was generally considered lucky to meet a toad, though to kill one brought on rain. Carrying a dead toad about with them was a sure way for criminals to escape detection, and no less effective as a preventive against epilepsy. Frogs were attributed similar powers, but a frog coming into a house was thought to be a bad omen. Girls often used frog bones in love divination:

> I do not want to hurt thee frog,
> But my true love's heart to turn,
> Wishing that he no rest may find,
> Till he come to me and speak his mind.

Fish were once believed to possess much wisdom and knowledge and to eat their flesh (more properly muscle) was to acquire some of that wisdom. Tench (sometimes called Dr Fish) were particularly sought after for curing the sick around Southport, in North Carolina. While at Bridlington, in England, and Newport Beach, California, fiddle-fish, although inedible, brought good luck for a year to the net, boat, fisherman or beachcomber that caught one.

Because Our Lord once rode on a donkey the hair of this beast is considered to have certain powers, especially if plucked from the cross-marking on its back. Even riding a donkey was said to cure many ills like toothache, whooping-cough and haemorrhoids. But in Devonshire, it was thought unlucky to walk on the ground on which a donkey had just rolled.

> Baldur rade. The foal slade (Slipped),
> He lighted, and he righted,
> Set joint to joint, and bone to bone,
> Sinew to sinew,
> Heal in Odin's name.

This piece of Scandinavian folk-lore from one of the oldest

animal superstitions known, refers to a ride of Odin and Baldur the Beautiful. When Baldur's horse slipped and broke its leg, Odin healed it immediately using a black thread tied in seven knots. As time went by the incantation was given a Christian context:

> The Lord rade. The foal slade.
> Set bone to bone,
> Sinew to sinew,
> Heal in the Holy Ghost's name.

Up to a few years ago, the black knotted thread was still being used as a cure for a poisoned thumb and other ailments in the Penzance area of Cornwall.

In Ireland, a white horse is thought to endow the owner with special skill in the curing of physical ills providing he is riding or driving the horse during the consultation. In the Andalusian district of Spain, a stag's horn tied up with hair from a mare's tail was said to have similar curative powers.

Horse hairs chopped finely and spread on bread and butter were once considered to be good for children, while schoolboys everywhere used to believe—and may still do—that if a horse hair was secreted in the palm of the hand during a caning, it would either split the cane, or save the victim from pain.

Not only was the horse believed to cure ills, but it was also credited with the gift of prophecy. Dean Swift meditated on this old belief in *A Voyage to the Houyhnhnms*, while William Camden in his *Britannia* hints at a similar superstition among the Saxons:

> ... the Saxons (were) very much addicted to superstition, and for that cause when they were to consult of weighty and important matters, besides soothsaying by inspection of beast's entrails, they observed especially the neighing of horses as presaging things to come. And thence perhaps it is that the Dukes of Saxonie in ancient times gave the horse (the power of Necromancy).

Among creatures of ill-omen, the weasel is near the top of the list, for witches were particularly addicted to taking its form. Its appearance near a house was a very unfortunate sign, and should the weasel squeak a death was imminent. Less disastrous, but indicative of certain misfortune, was if a weasel crossed anyone's path, particularly if it ran away to the left of the travel-ler. White weasels were especially feared because of their similarity to ghostly wraiths.

Mice have always been connected in folk-lore with visible manifestations of the soul and there are many tales of human souls leaving the body in sleep to enter and control mice. Issuing from the mouth of the subject, the ghost-mouse may wander far and wide at incredible speed, but should the sleeper be awakened before the soul-mouse has returned, that person will have lost his soul for ever.

Like mice, rats were also closely associated with the souls of men, but credited with more wisdom and some foreknowledge. Rats suddenly deserting a ship, for instance, was a warning of disaster, particularly if the ship had not yet left port, and it was considered an equally bad omen if rats were seen suddenly to leave a house.

Susceptible to music and magical choruses (remember the Pied Piper of Hamelyn in 1284), rats were serenaded to do the work of necromancers; while many an old legend tells of rats and mice employed as instruments of superstitious retribution: Asbjorn, the legendary Scandinavian earl, was eaten alive by rats for his murder of St Knut at Odense in 1086. Again, the evil Bishop Hatto of Mayence is said to have been pursued and killed by rats around AD 970 for his wilful murder by starvation of innocent parishioners.

Throughout the north of England and Scotland something like the following little rhyme was recited against a super-abundance of rats and mice:

> Ratton and mouse,
> Lea' the puir woman's house:

> Gang awa' over to 'e mill,
> And there a' ye'll get y're fill.

Moles, generally speaking, have been regarded as portents of good luck, though, in some districts, if a molehill appeared in a garden, it was believed to presage the death of an occupant of one of the neighbouring houses. Mole-blood has been used for healing warts, and mole-foot was a popular curative agent for rheumatism, gout and neuralgia.

Witches were said to turn themselves into hares by reciting this rhyme three times:

> I shall goe into an hare,
> With sorrow and such and much care;
> And I shall goe in the Devil's name
> Until I come home again.

Although it was a bad omen for a traveller to see a hare before setting out on a journey, in pagan times it was worshipped as a sacred animal and associated with fertility during the Spring Rites. The right foot of a hare, carried in the left-hand pocket, was deemed to keep rheumatism away. In his *Diary* for 25 March 1665, Samuel Pepys wrote: 'Now I am at a loss to know whether it be my hare's foot which is my preservative against wind, for I never had a fit of the collique since I wore it.'

Rabbits seem to have attracted similar superstitions to hares, neither of whose names should ever be mentioned while at sea. In the USA, the Easter Rabbit now rivals the European Easter Hare as a bringer of Easter Eggs.

Cows do not seem to have gathered as many superstitions around them as other animals, although as the companions of the Holy Family in the stable at Bethlehem, they were at one time thought blessed, and are still revered throughout India. Cow dung, too, has been widely credited with curative properties and poultices made from it are said to be particularly effective for the relief of pneumonia and similar ills.

Hedgehogs, when under the influence of witches, were popularly believed to steal milk from cows at night, a belief still firmly cherished by many country folk today. Cooked hedgehogs were also said to be good for eye troubles, and the animal was even better thought of as a weather diviner. Witness this from *Poor Robin's Almanac*:

> Observe which way the hedgehog builds her nest,
> To front the north or south, or east or west;
> For if 'tis true that common people say,
> The wind will blow quite contrary way.
> If by some secret art the hedgehogs know
> So long before, which way the winds will blow,
> She has an art which many a person lacks,
> That thinks himself fit to make almanacs.

Sheep have usually been deemed lucky animals and their bones have been kept for divination. A loud cacophony of sheep 'baas' was thought to precede rain, just as it is still generally believed that cows lie down in their pastures when settled weather is assured.

A cat's sneeze was commonly said to forecast rain, but a sick cat was pushed out of the house by some who averred that its sickness would 'invade the whole house'. To stroke a black cat's tail, however, was thought to cure a stye in the eye. Cats born in May were once thought most unlucky to have about the house and were usually drowned; it was alleged that they sucked babies' breath and suffocated them.

Another sure sign of rain was to have a snail cross one's path, while to touch one of its horns was to ensure lifelong good fortune. Snails have also been frequently credited with healing powers, particularly in the case of warts and for ear troubles. Snail-slime was once claimed as a cure for consumption, and even as late as 1929 there are records of people in the Blue Ridge Mountains of Virginia swallowing snails whole to cure tuberculosis.

From early times, butterflies have been associated with human souls, particularly in Egypt and Burma where the *win-laik-pya* varieties are thought to fly as ghost-souls. The newly dead were thought to inhabit butterflies for a while and to hover, semi-visible, over the corpse; a golden butterfly seen at a funeral spelt longevity for the mourners. Again, those who saw a white butterfly for the first time in summer were credited with luck throughout that year.

The fox, another animal closely associated with witches, was a lucky sign if seen alone; but a pack of foxes—understandably—was regarded as an ill-omen. There is a superstition that bears breed only once every seven years, causing disturbances in the atmosphere which make cattle in the vicinity lose their young. But children were said to have been cured of whooping-cough by riding on a bear.

As man's first servant and friend, the dog holds high place in superstition, being credited with the ability to see ghosts and hear sounds beyond human ken, and itself capable of be-coming a ghost after death. Such ghostly figures of dogs are usually said, by legend, to be guardians of some kind, and occasionally to appear in forewarning of a death in certain families. A dog that howled for no apparent reason was an ominous sign to the superstitious—and no doubt a confounded nuisance to the neighbours—but a piece of a dog's tongue hung round the neck could be a useful cure for scrofula.

Cats, too, have always figured prominently in superstition and were venerated in ancient Egypt. Though reputedly the familiars of witches, black cats are generally considered in Great Britain to be bringers of good luck, whereas the opposite view is more often taken in the United States, as in Belgium and Spain.

Beetles are bad omens if seen to crawl out of a shoe but spiders have generally been believed to bring good luck, as witness the rhyme: 'If you wish to live and thrive, let a spider run alive.' Spiders in a house foretold happiness and prosperity, and should one drop from the ceiling on to a person, it could be taken as the sign of a pending legacy. In ancient times, these creatures, and their webs, were swallowed whole as reputed cures for various ills like ague and jaundice.

Bees are associated with many old country superstitions, most of which are concerned with their alleged foreknowledge of future events. So greatly were they revered in pagan communities that to kill one was little short of sacrilege. Bees are also reputed to be unable to live near a house in which there is anger or hatred, and to be particularly averse from swearing and blasphemy. If a girl was a virgin she was thought to be able to pass safely through a swarm of bees, and it was for long a common custom in Britain to 'inform' the bees when their master had died; the hives were struck three times with an old iron key and told of the death, sometimes in rhyme.

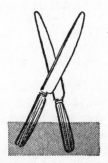

9

Birds of Good and Evil Omen

Because they were supposed to fly around crying 'Bewitched', lapwings were once considered birds of ill-omen and legend claimed that the souls of men doomed never to find rest lived on in the bodies of lapwings.

Traditionally foretelling the coming of summer, the swallow was associated with fertility and water. Even today it is a very good sign if a swallow builds its nest on a house, for that house, so it is said, will be immune from damage by fire or lightning. In Germany and Scotland, by contrast, the swallow was known as the Devil's servant and a bird the sign of which brought not good luck but only poverty. However, dead it still had its uses, its flesh being said to improve the eyesight, cure palsy and relieve kidney trouble.

A widespread superstition in Great Britain and Ireland during the Middle Ages was that barnacle geese were born on timbered wrecks at the bottom of the sea. Thus considered more fish than fowl, it was permissible to eat goose during Lent. Giraldus Cambrensis leaves us their interesting gestation story in his *Topographia Hibernicae* of 1186:

> (They) are produced from fir timber tossed along the sea and are at first like gum. Afterwards they hang down by their beaks as if they were seaweed attached to the timber, and are surrounded by shells in order to grow more freely. Having thus in the process of time been clothed with a strong coat of feathers, they either fall into the water or fly freely away into the air. They derive their food and growth from the sap of the wood or from the sea, by a secret and most wonderful process of alimentation. I have frequently seen, with my own eyes, more than a thousand of these small birds hanging down on the sea shore from one piece of timber, enclosed in their shells and already formed. They do not breed and lay eggs like other birds, nor do they ever hatch any eggs, nor do they seem to build nests in any corner of the earth. Hence bishops and religious men in some parts of Ireland do not scruple to dine off these birds at the time of fasting, because they are not flesh nor born of flesh.

A bird of many legends is the cock, considered almost universally as a sun-bird and the enemy of ghosts and spirits. Once sacred to the gods of war, the cock was said to have been the herald of Christ's birth and one superstition had it that all cocks, including the metal and wooden ones on church spires and towers, would crow loudly on the Last Day to awaken the dead. A cock crowing at midnight was taken to mark the passing of a spirit, and if it crowed three times at this house the Angel of Death himself was about. Cocks crowing at a house door foretold the coming of strangers and if one perched on a gate to crow at night the next day would surely be wet.

A white cock was considered very lucky, but black cocks had an ominous significance as particular favourites of the Devil.

In France, the credulous would take a black cock at midnight to a cross-roads and shout *Poule noire a vendre*: whereupon, it was supposed, the Devil would appear, claim the cock and leave a heap of gold coins in exchange.

Sometimes cocks were used to detect criminals. The birds would be placed in an upturned bucket and the suspects lined up before it. Each had to touch the bucket rim in turn, and the cock would crow at the touch of the guilty person. Hungarian bridal processions, at one time, were preceded by a man leading a cock to invoke good fortune for the young people.

Symbols of the Resurrection and resurgent life, eggs have a special place in superstition and it has for long been an Easter tradition to bring good luck by exchanging eggs which have been coloured by dyes. Called Pace-eggs, one at least was set aside in many households to ensure the luck continuing throughout the year. In some parts, however, it was considered unlucky to bring any kind of egg indoors and some old-time sailors would never mention them by name at sea.

, Eggs were often used by witches, as proved by an entry in the parish registers of Wells-next-the-Sea in Norfolk, England, in the year 1583. There it is recorded that fourteen men were damned to drowning 'by the detestable working of an execrable witche of King's Lynn, whose name was Mother Gabley . . . by the boiling or rather labouring of certayn Eggs in a payle full of colde water, afterwards proved sufficiently at ye arraignment of ye said Witche'.

With its proud demeanour, the peacock has always been considered a royal bird and was sacred to many cultures. The most common superstition about this bird is that it is unlucky to have its tail feathers in the house, no doubt because the 'open eye' marks on these feathers were associated with the Evil Eye. Swans are better known in legend than superstition, though it was once considered to be courting misfortune to kill one as they were supposed to be re-incarnated human souls. Another tradition claimed that swans could only hatch their eggs during a storm and sang at their best just before they died—hence perhaps the origin of the term 'swansong'.

Owls, like almost all night birds, have always been objects of superstitious fear. Although dreaded in Roman times as an omen of death, the owl was revered in Greece as the bird of Athene, Goddess of Wisdom, since when wisdom and the owl seem to have become synonymous.

An owl perching on a house is said to be an omen of death, and in Ireland an owl entering a house is immediately killed, the superstition being that should it be released it will take with it all the house's good fortune. Another bird of ill-omen, the nightjar, is said to embody the spirits of babies who died unbaptised. In Latin, the nightjar is called *Caprimulgus* (goat-milker), the belief being that they suck the udders of goats and destroy their sight.

Sacred to Odin, the raven is often distrusted as a 'spy', no doubt because of the old Norse myth about Odin's two birds, Hugin and Munin, which were said to have flown over the world each day and reported all the things they had seen to their master. Because it eats carrion, the raven is also associated with war and destruction, and to hear one croak near a sick bed augurs the imminent death of the ailing; to eat the flesh of the raven, however, is said to help cure blindness. Scottish deer-stalkers believe it is lucky to hear a raven croak before setting out on a hunt, and a well-known superstition about the ravens at the Tower of London is that should the birds die out, or fly away, the reigning royal house would fall, and Britain with it.

It is still believed most unlucky to kill or maim a robin, and it is said that even cats seem to respect this superstition, and very rarely harm robins. The best known legend to account for the robin's red breast is that on the first Good Friday, the robin tried to draw a thorn from Christ's crown of thorns and was stained with His blood. Both in Wales and Oxfordshire it is considered a death omen, or at least a herald of bad news, for a robin to sit on a window-sill and sing. And, according to J. A. Lupton in his *A Thousand Notable Things* (1660), 'a Robyn read breast, fynding the dead body of a man or woman, wyll cover the face of the same with Mosse'.

During the days of sail, an albatross flying round a ship in mid-ocean was a sure sign of stormy weather. These birds were held to embody the spirits of dead mariners, and a sailor who killed an albatross could expect to be dogged by ill-luck for the rest of his life. Samuel Taylor Coleridge (1772–1834) incorporated the superstition in his poem *The Ancient Mariner*:

> At length did cross an Albatross
> Through the fog it came;
> As if it had been a Christian soul,
> We hailed it in God's name.
> God save thee ancient Mariner!
> From the fiends that plague thee thus!
> Why look'st thou so? With my cross-bow
> I shot the Albatross.
> I had done an hellish thing,
> And it would work 'em woe:
> For all averred, I had killed the bird
> That made the breezes blow.

For his crime, the mariner who shot the albatross was condemned by his mates to have the rotting carcass tied around his neck.

The appearance of a large number of waxwings is considered a portent of war, and the magpie, too, is a bird of ill-omen which owes its black and white plumage to its refusal to go into full mourning at the Crucifixion. To encounter a magpie while on a journey was considered ominous, and misfortune could only be averted if a martin was sighted soon afterwards.

Two other black-coloured birds superstitiously associated with bad luck are jackdaws and crows when seen alone, and when either crows or rooks were seen tumbling in the air like acrobats it was said to be a sign of coming rain and high winds.

The cuckoo, like the swallow a herald of spring, is the subject of several country superstitions, all associated with misfortune of some kind, whereas the colourful kingfisher has a much happier reputation and its feathers, sewn into clothes, were firmly believed to serve as a life protector.

The cry of the curlew, if heard at night, was said to foretell a nearby disaster, while the eagle, it was believed, could impart some of the powers of its 'eagle eye' to sufferers from failing eyesight if they ate of the bird's gall mixed—happily for them—with honey.

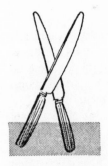

IO

Secret Wisdom of Proverbs and Folk-lore

Proverbs, like folk-song and ballads, are often the only remaining hints we have of old superstitions and are thus significant contributions to social history. Often used as mnemonics for superstitions, proverbs are world-wide in their origins and range from the ancient Egyptian *Precepts of Ptah-hotep* (*c* 2500 BC) to the English *Proverbs of Alfred* (*c* 1150–80), and from the American *Poor Richard's Almanac* (1732–57) to the *Proverbes dramatique* of Alfred de Musset (1810–57).

Here are a few which perpetuate old superstitions:

> He who bathes in May will soon be
> laid in clay; he who bathes in June
> will sing a merry tune; he who bathes
> in July, will dance like a fly.

Bathing has always been considered a ritual of magical significance, men believing that they could free themselves from physical and spiritual states simply by washing, and also bring harm to themselves by washing at unfavourable times. Guilt, pain and taboos of various kinds have all been removed to the satisfaction of the superstitious by ceremonial ablutions, Pontius Pilate setting an early example of his own.

Some people abstained from ever washing at all not from laziness but for fear of washing their luck away—miners in Wales, for instance, were careful not to wash their backs for fear that if they did the pit roof would fall in on them. Men working in abattoirs ceremonially washed their blood-guilt away, but were careful to do so alone as it was thought that two people washing in the same water were certain to quarrel immediately afterwards. Others held that strife could be averted if one of them spat in the water after washing.

Woe to him that has a priest in his kin.

Even today some sailors would feel ill at ease if they saw a clergyman immediately before starting a voyage, and the word 'minister' should never be mentioned on board ship. The ill luck which was for long associated with having a clergyman on board as a passenger became such a prevalent superstition at one time that Bishop Bartholomew Iscanus of Exeter ordained penalties in his *Poenitentiale* against such beliefs. But sailors, of course, have always been notoriously superstitious, dreading to start a voyage on a Friday and firmly believing that to change a ship's name was to bring inevitable bad luck.

> The bairn that is born on fair Sunday
> Is bonny and loving, and blithe and gay.
> Monday's bairn is fair in the face,
> Tuesday's bairn is full of grace.
> Wednesday's bairn is loving and giving,
> Thursday's bairn works hard for a living.
> Friday's bairn is a child of woe,
> Saturday's bairn has far to go.
>
> (A proverb from Massachusetts)

106

It is a very ancient belief that the day of one's birth influenced one's life pattern and there are various versions of this proverb in different parts of the world. The phase of the moon at the time of birth was held to be of particular significance, especially among coast-line communities where the ebb and flow of the tides was an important factor in their daily lives.

If two knives are crossed today have a care at work and play.

Crossing knives, like spilling salt, has always been said to bring bad luck, as is toasting bread with the point of a knife, or spinning a knife on a table.

> When a picture leaves the wall
> Someone then receives a call.

Many believed that a picture falling from a wall foretold a sudden death in a family.

> If you see a pin and let it lie
> You'll need a pin before you die.

Pins have always been essential items in a witch's equipment, especially for casting spells; all a witch needed to do to make someone bow to her will was to burn twelve pins on the fire at midnight while chanting this spell: ' 'Tis not these pins I wish to burn, but —'s heart I wish to turn. May he neither sleep nor rest, till he has granted my request.' And a crooked pin should always be left alone in case you pick up sorrow.

> A whistling girl doth rouse the Devil.

Which is probably why Cornish miners believed that to whistle underground in a mine attracted malignant spirits, and why whistling in a theatre is considered most unlucky by actors, who believe that it is inviting a premature end to the run of a play. Sailors, too, are chary about whistling on board, though in sailing ships it was permissible in a flat calm as a proven method of summoning a favourable wind.

> You should on Candlemas Day (2 February) throw
> candle and candlestick away.

Once the chief source of household light, the candle inevitably became the subject of a number of superstitions. Sparks from the wick once foretold the coming of strangers, a wavy flame where there was no draught meant high winds, a blue flame prophesied frost, and a candle which was difficult to light was an indication of rain to come.

Those who lit a candle from a fire in the hearth could expect to die in a workhouse, and a candle allowed to burn out on its own or left in an empty room were equal invitations to bad luck.

Candles were also once used for death curses; the name of the intended victim was written down the length of a candle, the belief being that as the wick burnt away each letter in the wax the person named become progressively weaker until death came as the last letter melted.

> When your nose is itching, watch out for a change of
> luck.

One of the several old superstitions, this, associated with similar bodily discomforts, such as that of any tingling sensation in the ears, meant that someone was talking about you, in the eyes a pleasant surprise, and in the feet that a journey was soon to be undertaken.

> If Easter falls on Lady Day, beware O' England.

The Feast of the Annunciation of the Virgin Mary (25 March) is commonly called Lady Day, and it was believed that if either Good Friday or Easter Sunday should fall on that day (believed to be the day on which the Crucifixion took place) England would suffer a great tragedy before twelve months had passed. In 1910, Good Friday fell on Lady Day and in May of that year King Edward VII died; in 1951, Easter Sunday fell on Lady Day and eleven months later King George VI died.

Better the last smile than the first laughter.

Laughter before breakfast, it was said, meant tears before evening, and those addicted to singing in their bath were similarly warned that:

If you sing before breakfast you'll cry before night.

Meet on the stairs and you won't meet in Heaven,

epitomised the popular superstition that it meant bad luck to both when two people met on the stairs, though it might be averted if the fingers of the right hand were crossed in passing. Falling up a staircase was lucky but falling down, as well as bringing its own prompt and painful proof of ill luck, was also deemed an ill-omen, especially at the beginning of a journey or the inception of a new project. Crossing the fingers is also, of course, an essential precaution against ill luck when passing under a ladder.

Some weather superstitions:

St Bartholomew brings the cold dew.

Dew has always had a magical reputation and was much used in charms and spells for sore eyes and skin troubles. In Scotland, May dew gathered in the early morning was the most potent for wishing spells.

Find the end of a rainbow and you will find a crock of gold.

This is a well-known old Irish superstition, but at one time the rainbow was considered to be Odin's bridge from the realm of man (Midgard) to the home of the gods (Asgard), and many cultures still look upon the rainbow as a bridge for souls.

If it rains on St Mary's Day (2 July) it will rain for four weeks.

Superstitions about rain abound, the most popular being

the one concerning St Swithin, the divine, who died in AD 862:

St Swithin's Day, if thou be fair,
For forty days 'twill rain nae mair;
St Swithin's Day, if thou be rain,
For forty days it will remain.

II

Gamblers' Luck

Gamblers in general are notoriously superstitious and take more than average care to try and avoid a run of bad luck.

The six most popular lucky objects carried around by gamblers at Monte Carlo were said to be: locks of hair, animal bones, 'holy' relics, four-leaved clovers, hooves and coins. At the turn of the century, however, superstitious gamblers thought it sufficient to have a pretty girl stand beside them for luck, and for the same reason Edwardian gamblers used to pay chorus girls to sit with them at the tables.

An old superstition connected with Monte Carlo concerned the statue of a bronze horse which stood outside the main entrance of the Hotel de Paris, beside the National Sporting Club. The knee-joint of this horse was thought to bring good luck, and many gamblers touched it on their way to the Casino. In fact, so many people stroked it that it became highly polished and a new manager at the hotel, unaware of the superstition, had the knee painted over. The response was immediate and old patrons threatened to boycott the hotel until he removed the paint!

Las Vegas and Reno, both in the State of Nevada, share the dubious honour of being the two places on earth with the highest number of superstitions in ratio of population. Here are a number of the most prevalent superstitions admitted to by professional gamblers; some of which no doubt date back to the days when gamblers plied the stage-coach lines and river steamers.

It is thought unlucky to play cards at a table without covering, and a green cover is thought to be the most auspicious. On encountering a run of bad luck, some players believe they can break the sequence by getting up and walking once round the table or their chairs.

A cross-eyed man seen at a casino is said to be a sign of good luck for the bank, whereas an old Monte Carlo superstition says that, following the suicide of an unlucky player, those who play against the bank will win.

Some gamblers say that it is unlucky to pick up cards until the dealer has finished, and that for good fortune chips should be kept in a neat pile and not scattered on the table. Sticking a pin into the lapel of a friend's coat is thought to bring a winning hand before a large bet but to borrow money during a session, or for a black card to fall on the floor during a game, is to court bad luck.

Most gamblers have a favourite card which they believe brings them good luck and, before starting a game, will try to touch it with the index finger before they sit down to play. But nobody loves the four of clubs, known as 'the Devil's bedstead', which is considered by many to be the unluckiest card in the pack.

Another curious superstition which has intrigued historians for centuries is the persistent belief that the nine of diamonds is the 'Curse of Scotland'. The most popular explanation for this is that the card was used by Sir John Dalrymple, Earl of Stair, to convey instructions for the massacre of the Macdonalds at Glencoe, a pass in Argyllshire, in 1692.

A run of black spade cards has been regarded as an omen of death or disaster for almost as long as playing cards have been invented. Mary, Queen of Scots, is said to have had her execution forecast by spade cards, and when playing cards the day before his death on Coniston Water, Donald Campbell turned up the ace of spades followed by the queen of the same suit.

Coincidences, of course, but the very essence of what superstition thrives upon.

12

Superstitions of the Professions

Superstition is not usually associated with officials in local government but those at Whittington, near Oswestry, in Shropshire, were recently faced with something of a dilemma. An Elizabethan sea-chest of considerable value was offered to the local council as an historical relic for permanent public display on condition that it should never be opened, the family superstition being that if the chest were opened the owner's heir would die. The council agreed to honour the condition, and doubtless hope that no inquisitive locksmith will ever be tempted to imperil the future succession of the donor's heir.

Acting is a profession notoriously addicted to superstition and members of most theatre companies believe it to be unlucky to have candles on stage, or in the dressing-room, and equally unlucky to look in a mirror over the shoulder of another. No actor in his senses would ever kick a cat, for it is a sign of good fortune to have one around the theatre. But for a cat to run across the stage during a performance is a certain indication of misfortune to follow.

Rehearsals, too, have their special superstitions, and as perfect ones are thought to prejudice the success of the first night, the last line of the dialogue or last bar of music is often left unsaid or unplayed just for luck.

The pantomime *Cinderella* is looked upon as a lucky one, whereas *Babes in the Wood* and *Robin Hood* are ill-starred. Certain songs, too, are taboo for some players: 'I Dreamt I Dwelt in Marble Halls' from *The Bohemian Girl* is one, and Tosti's 'Good-bye' is another. For similarly superstitious reasons the witches' song in *Macbeth* is associated with misfortune, and the play itself has been blamed for numerous disasters at theatres, accidents to actors, fires and flops.

Many actors believe that real flowers on stage are unlucky and prefer imitations. Peacock feathers or any representation of a peacock on stage are to be avoided at all costs but should an actor's shoes squeak as he steps on stage he can count upon a good reception.

Individual actors and actresses, of course, have their own superstitions. Al Jolson never wore new clothes on opening night and Monique van Dooren keeps a lucky black dress near at hand when doing a show. Carole Lombard is said to have carried a smooth round pebble for luck, a gift from Clark Gable. Pat O'Brien favoured four-leaved clovers, and George Brent put his faith in an old Irish shilling. Cecil B. de Mille wore riding breeches for luck, and Bette Davis relied so much on a charm in the form of a gold beetle that 'curtain up' was liable to be delayed when she mislaid the trinket.

Superstition was once a large part of a doctor's stock-in-trade, and while many people believed that 'free' medicine would not work, others often kept a few pence back from the doctor's bill, considering it unlucky to pay in full. It is still thought unlucky by some to call in a doctor on a Friday and, according to another superstition, the seventh child of a seventh child who takes up medicine as a profession will surpass all others in talent.

Politicians, too, have their pet superstitions but none could surpass the former Canadian Premier, Mackenzie King, who was said by his friends to have a superstition for every hour of the day. A close runner-up was Charles Stewart Parnell, the Irish statesman who considered the colour green (usually lucky for Irishmen) to be deadly for him.

Many business men avoid certain 'unlucky' days for signing contracts, and keep old neckties, buttons, pens and pencils for luck; in the US, new business ventures are usually sent horse-shoe floral gifts by well-wishers.

Tradesmen, craftsmen and sportsmen all have their own particular superstitions. Some bakers were credited with the ability to make cakes which would enable the eater to glimpse the future. Called 'Dumb Cakes', they were particularly popular at the year's end with unmarried women. Bakers also used to sprinkle salt around the bakery for good fortune, but anyone else who spilt it was inviting bad luck unless a pinch was thrown three times over the left shoulder.

Because they were concerned with such mystic elements as fire and water, blacksmiths figure in many country superstitions. Much feared in certain countries (a hymn, 'St Patrick's Breastplate', was sung to invoke God's protection against 'spells of women, smiths and druids'), blacksmiths were often credited with powers to heal ailments in human beings as well as in horses. Some, known as 'bloodcharmers', could stop bleeding by simple touch.

As for sportsmen, boxer Bob Fitzsimmons always kept a horseshoe nailed up at his training camp for good luck, while Georges Carpentier would not dream of entering the ring unless his manager was wearing a certain coat which he regarded as his mascot. Ezzard Charles kept a lucky dress belonging to his wife near him whenever he had a fight.

Foolish and credulous perhaps, but who does not cherish a superstition or two of his own even if he may not admit it—or even recognise it as such!

Index